GRIT TO GLORY
Raising the 13 Armoured

GRIT TO GLORY

Raising the 13 Armoured

Brig. B. S. Mehta

OCCAM | An Imprint of BluOne Ink

Title: Grit to Glory: Raising the 13 Armoured
Author: Brig. B. S. Mehta

ISBN: 978-93-92209-29-1
Edition: 1

Published by:
BluOne Ink LLP
Imprint: Occam

Publisher's Address:
306, Tower-I, Assotech Business Cresterra,
Plot No. 22, Sector 135, Noida.

Website: www.bluone.ink
Email: publisher@bluone.ink

Printed in India at Thomson Press (India) Ltd.

OCCAM | An Imprint of **BluOne Ink**

To my wife, Jayshree, and our children,
Brijraj and Nandini

Contents

Preface

Ever since we have known of armies, the commanding officer has been regarded as the most important link in the chain of command. He is responsible for training his men for war as well as their welfare. His personality is reflected in his unit, and his authority remains unchallenged. A commanding officer epitomizes a true patriot who loves, trains and leads his unit to defend their country and its interests, perennially prepared for the ultimate sacrifice of their life for the nation. It is for this reason that military service is considered the most honourable.

Grit to Glory: Raising the 13 Armoured reflects the tradition, culture and professionalism of our Armed Forces, which the regiment imbibed during the period of its raising. The high sense of elan and panache reflected in its ability to rapidly adapt to the concepts of mobile warfare of a Strike Corps and win recognition for its performance under battle-like conditions is a tribute to the officers and men who raised the 13 Armoured. To raise an Armoured Regiment, command it in combat, serve as its Colonel and then watch it grow nearly four decades later is an astounding experience of a lifetime, one that makes me extremely nostalgic.

I vividly recall how in the immediate aftermath of Operation Blue Star, I was reverted from the Research & Analysis Wing (RAW) to raise 13 Armoured Regiment (13 AR) by General A. S. Vaidya, Chief of the Army Staff, in 1984. The unit was assigned a unique class composition of Sikh, Rajput and South Indian Classes—a first in India's cherished military history. It was equipped with the defect-prone indigenous Vijayanta tank and the moniker 13 laced with superstition.

This was the first unit being raised after 1971. A positive mindset and the untapped, raw potential of the rank and file along with the officers posted out of the existing armoured regiments became our only asset. The number 13 drew early inspiration from Guru Nanak Dev's *Tehra Sab Tera*, which pushed us to mould ourselves into a regiment 'fit for war', that too within a stipulated time, while also instilling pride by developing its badge, flag and motto *Veer Bhogya Vasundhara.*

Selected for participating in the Republic Day Parade at New Delhi and Allahabad, the regiment was mobilized under Operation Trident to form part of the Reorganized Army Plains Infantry Division (RAPID) under 2 Corps deployed in the desert for Exercise Brasstacks. Pakistan's Zia-ul-Haq unleashed Operation Sledgehammer and had his Army Reserves deployed on the Punjab border to counter perceived threat posed to their nascent nuclear installation. The media on both sides had hyped the imminence of war between the neighbours. It is in the midst of such trying circumstances that the officers of 13 AR exhibited exemplary courage, comradeship and entrepreneurial innovation to make use of the resources at their disposal and put their best foot forward. That spirit continues to resound in their hearts even after all these years.

This work is not just an attempt to bookmark their individual as well as collective journeys with 13 AR but also to help the civilian ascertain the raw tenacity of a soldier, who is willing to go the extra mile to comply, to make things happen, no matter what. Therein lies glory!

I am delighted that the book is being published this year, a year that carries special significance as it bears witness to another important change—the first directly commissioned officer of the regiment, Second Lieutenant Shailjanand Jha, having grown with the regiment to reach the rank of Major General, will on retirement hand over the responsibilities as Colonel of the regiment to Brigadier

B. S. Bisht, who has previously commanded 13 AR with distinction. The change augurs well for the regiment as the interests of the regiment are best served when those officers who have commanded it, take on the mantle of Colonelcy.

Acknowledgements

A few weeks before Covid-19 was declared a pandemic, my wife, Jayshree, decided to lock up our flat in Gurugram and move to our home in Dharamshala, Kangra. This turned out to be a wise decision as the distress and anguish caused by Covid-19 was mortifying, to say the least. Moving to the salubrious, pollution-free, invigorating Dhauladhar encouraged me to put pen to paper to make this book a reality. My first thanks goes out to Jayshree.

The presence of my children, Brijraj and Nandini, was a blessing. They were always around to read my rough drafts, help me with the complexities of the computer and listen to the same story with patience. As I spent long hours at the desk, they drove down to Pathankot to add a new member to the family—a bull mastiff pup named Trigger. The growing demands of Trigger kept me occupied and also ensured that I took ample breaks from the computer. These frequent walks with Trigger became opportunities to reflect and recall the raising of 13 AR. Their affection contributed to the writing while their criticism provided balance to the narration.

I received unparalleled support from Colonel Neeraj Naithani, Colonel Nitish Patial and Colonel Piyush Verma, the current commandant, who responded to every request for old letters/ references/ photographs with dispatch, with assistance from their clerical staff working in the Regimental Headquarters. I must add a special word of thanks to Major General S. N. Jha, PVSM, VSM, Colonel Shashank Yadav, Colonel Virender Singh, Colonel Manbir Singh, who all responded in helping me recall the finer details of a journey we took over four decades ago.

A special thanks to Colonel Mir Ahmed Shah and Colonel V. K. Kochhar, who shared the notes and extracts from their personal diaries without the need to edit portions critical of their commanding officer. These have been quoted in the text. Colonel Umesh Varma was generous enough to share photographs from his private collection and helped in writing the captions. A few veterans were also kind enough to respond to my call for photographs along with others like Major Ajay Arora, Major Pradeep Samyal, Colonel Anil Pandit, Lieutenant General Ajay Gupta, Colonel Sarab Butalia, Colonel Aman Oberoi, Lieutenant Colonel Dhruv Saraswat, Major S. D. Syal, Major Daksh Dhankar, Lieutenant Colonel Chetan Mahapatra, Major Akhil Bhaskar and Major Vineet Choudhary.

I must also thank Colonel Bhupinder Singh (14H/45C), an established author and artist for helping recreate the LAW-87 sketch sent as feedback to General Hanut Singh after Exercise Brasstacks.

A special mention must be made of Late Lieutenant Colonel Randhir Singh, who had expressed happiness on learning about this book. He was a pillar of strength and a dear friend who would have enjoyed reading the book. I could say the same for the late Colonel K. K. Chowdhury, a spirited officer of 13 AR, who was also a founding member. May their souls rest in peace.

Lastly, I am indebted to BluOne Ink for the fine team that they have put together for publishing my book. Their sense of propriety, invaluable suggestions and high standards of excellence have added value to my book. My special thanks to Garima Syal, my editor, for many valuable suggestions. Mature advice from Mini Narayanan and design inputs from Prachi Kishore and Mansi Pawar were extremely beneficial for the book, not to forget Pankaj P. Singh, whose close coordination works well for BluOne Ink.

13

Armoured Regiment

A 13-point Fact File

1. **Raised on:** 21 December 1984
2. **Raised by:** Lieutenant Colonel Balram Singh Mehta (Retired as Brigadier)
3. **Composition:** Fixed class comprising Sikh, Rajput and South Indian Classes. 13 AR is India's only armoured regiment raised with such a class composition.
4. **Type:** Division Regiment Armoured Corps
5. **Size:** Armoured Regiment
6. **Equipment:** Vijayanta tanks, later upgraded to T-90S tanks
7. **Regimental Motto:** *Veer Bhogya Vasundhara* (The brave shall inherit the Earth.)
8. **Regimental Insignia:** The cap badge of the unit is a sunburst with crossed lances and pennons of traditional cavalry. The regimental motto is inscribed on a circlet within the sunburst as a horseshoe with '13' embossed inside. The original design was mined from the salient features of the badges of famous armoured regiments like President's Body Guard (PBG), 16 Light Cavalry (16C), 1 Skinner's Horse (1H), 17 Poona Horse (17H), 45 Cavalry (45C) to weave together a unique design that was distinctive and appealing. The shoulder title consists of the numeral '13' in brass.
9. **Regimental Flag:** The tank-fired shell, scarlet red, is shown penetrating the grey enemy armour, splitting it wide open after destruction. This reflects the cornerstone of the regiment's philosophy and its tank commanders and crews to remain focused and determined to penetrate and destroy the enemy's

armour, while remembering the basic training of *'ek gola, ek dushmun'.*

10. **First Flag Hoisting:** 16 March 1985
11. **First Exercise with Troops:** Exercise Shakti Vallabh
12. **First All Arms Exercise:** First major combined arms military exercise, Exercise Brasstacks of the Indian Armed Forces in Rajasthan in March 1987
13. **Battle-Ready:** While participating in the Republic Day Parade at two separate geographical centres, the regiment was mobilized at short notice under Operation Trident and inducted into 14 Strike RAPID Formation of India's Strike Corps, deployed in the desert. The officers and men of 13 Armoured Regiment had not been trained to operate in the desert. However, they used their ingenuity and skill to prepare for battle to participate in mobile warfare under General Hanut, GOC 2 Corps, which helped the regiment establish a unique identity within the Armoured Corps.

Prologue

It was the month of October in 1984. I was inside a tent replacement hut made from prefabricated cement slabs with corrugated sheets on the roof—the Indian Army's interim answer to cover an overall shortage of accommodation for troops in peace stations. A dim light bulb hung from the roof while a creaky fan, moving at agonizing speed, circulated the damp, musty air. The only window was still shut as if the TRH block had been lying unused for a considerable period. A large table had been laid out for lunch with six chairs on either side. The crockery, cutlery and silverware had been arranged as in a regular army mess. The decorations were perfect. On the table, I could see a candlestand with 13 candles burning bright. The flickering light was reflected from the sides of silver trophies on display. On the side wall was a banner which read: Welcome to your Regiment! Many of the officers had arrived, dressed in jackets and ties. I could overhear someone talking in a hushed tone, 'Sir, one more officer is coming.' The light inside was hazy, and the faces appeared blurred. I was standing at the head of the table, my hands resting on a chair. In front of me lay an open invitation card that announced: Lunch at 1313 hours. Also on display was the menu card with a large number '13' embossed on top of a long list. I suspected this could also be the total number of dishes prepared. The door opened and a man in uniform, wearing three stripes of a dafadar on his left shoulder, marched up to an officer and announced lunch: '*Bhojan taiyar hai, Shriman.*' (The meal is served.) The person who took the report appeared stressed due to the long delay imposed by the latecomer. He was tall, with an impressive moustache and a throaty voice. There was complete silence as the non-commissioned officer (NCO) clicked his heels and turned around to go out from the same door he had used to come in. Before he could cross the threshold, the person who took the report broke the ominous silence with his gruff voice, '*Bhejo kisi ko, bolo 12 officer unka intezar kar rahe hain.*' (Send someone; 12 officers are waiting for him.) The NCO, who had momentarily stopped to receive the instructions, was still in the doorway when the door swung open. 'Sir, *Butalia Saab aa gaye.*' (Sir, Butalia saheb is here.) A tall Sikh with a clipped beard was apologising profusely for the delay; his voice was droopy. The NCO banged the door shut as he rushed out.

I got up with a tremor. It was still early dawn outside. On the desk, across the room, I could recognize my Senior Command notebook. Yes, I was in Mhow, a small town near Indore, with its Army War College, recovering from an early morning dream. Now who was Butalia? I could not remember him, just the name lingered on. The memory faded as I got busy with the morning prayers.

A few days before the completion of the Senior Command Course, orders had arrived for my attachment to the Centre and School (ACC&S), Ahmednagar. It ended with a terse message: Further orders will follow. As per grapevine, this attachment was temporary and would lapse soon after the government's approval for raising a new armoured regiment at Ahmednagar was sanctioned. One of the officers from the Military Secretary branch, who was attending the same course, had tipped me off in strict confidence that a proposal to nominate me as Commandant of a new raising, 13 Armoured Regiment, had the approval of the Chief of Army Staff (COAS). I was neither surprised nor disillusioned at this development after my baneful meeting with General A. S. Vaidya, COAS, at New Delhi before reverting from the Research and Analysis Wing of the Cabinet Secretariat. It was only a matter of a few weeks for the formal orders to be issued, assigning me as Commandant-Designate of a new armoured regiment. As an officer who had voluntarily re-joined his regiment before the declaration of the 1971 war and had subsequently been decorated for gallantry during the Tank versus Tank Battle of Garibpur, I could lay claim to command 45 Cavalry, the regiment I went to war with. In the words of a senior officer, the MS branch policy could not overlook that I was mentioned in despatches for my combat service during the 1971 war. My claim would not count for much as it had been approved by the COAS, who was also the Colonel of the regiment. I was, in reality, left with a Hobson's choice. The milder and more dignified consolation was to accept that whatever happens, happens for the good. Instead of pointing fingers or raising questions of propriety on those regimental officers who were advising the Colonel of the regiment, the pragmatic option was to prepare for the reality as it was unfolding. Quite like my father, I could draw some consolation from 'If' by Rudyard Kipling:

And lose, and start again at your beginnings,
And never breathe a word about your loss.

1

Early Life

The partition of India in 1947 left my family with no choice but to abandon home and hearth, to 'lose, and start again' at the 'beginnings'[1] . My family members, friends and distant kin suffered the indignities of violence, assault, plunder and exploitation that most refugees were exposed to. We were still luckier though—we lived through the trauma of the partition without the humiliation of spending time in refugee camps, like thousands of other less fortunate people. My father's Defence Accounts office had been relocated from Rawalpindi to Shree Sahoo Palace, Pune (then Poona) a little before the mayhem and massacres had started. My earliest memory of the partition is that of a refugee train—wagonloads of refugees, many hanging from the overcrowded roofs of railway wagons and coaches, descending like a swarm of flies on arrival at the station. I had accompanied my father to receive a family arriving by this train. A frail, dishevelled middle-aged man, holding his *pagri* and a satchel in his hand, broke into tears on meeting us. I am 77

[1] From If by Rudyard Kipling

years old now. In the intervening years, I have scratched my mind and memory, but this remains my first and only recollection of the traumatic year of 1947.

We are a family of Mohiyal Brahmins from Bhaun, district Jhelum, in what is now Pakistan. The surname Mehta is a title granted to the more erudite and better educated among the community. The Mohiyal Brahmins are associated with Maharaja Hari Singh's family of Kashmir, who was himself a Mohiyal Brahmin. This community has a tradition of soldiering from the time when Alexander invaded India. The Mohiyals had developed their reputation as sentinels of India's borders and their chivalry was recognized by the Mughals and the British. The Mohiyals developed a warlike culture and reputation comparable to the Pashtuns and Rajputs and were the only non-Muslim group to carry the titles of 'Khan' and 'Sultan'. Many Mohiyals who resided in the military belt of Cambelpur, Rawalpindi and Jhelum served in cavalry regiments; mostly 9, 11, 13, 19 Lancers and 3, 4, 15 Guides Cavalry. During the 1971 war, several one-, two- and three-star Mohiyal generals, marshals and admirals had led Indian troops into Pakistan.

My father, F. C. Mehta, having participated in the Afghan War in which he was commended for gallantry, later joined the Indian Defence Accounts Service (IDAS)[2]. Before the partition, he moved to Shree Sahoo Palace, near the Bund Garden, in Pune as the Chief Administrative Officer in mid-1947 along with my mother, Sheila, and their three children, Shamsher, myself and Kusum. An old faithful staff, Gangadhar, a stout Nepalese, had accompanied us from Pakistan. Father's hobbies included poetry, gardening, palmistry and homoeopathy. This made him a popular figure in the large Shree Sahoo Palace Complex that served as an office-cum-residence. It had sprawling lawns, a well-maintained garden

[2] Later became Indian Audit and Accounts Service (IAAS)

and a circular water tank with a fountain facing a double-storied house. A black Morris Minor stood parked in the garage. I have vivid memories of my father walking in the garden with a white shawl wrapped around his shoulders or sitting in his private dispensary, dishing out free homoeopathic medicines to families of staff members. He was a qualified homoeopath, having earned a diploma in his younger days. He was a great admirer of the famous singer K. L. Saigal. Amongst his favourite songs were '*Duniya mein hoon duniya ka talabgar nahi hoon*', '*Jab dil hi toot gaya*' and '*Babul mora*'.

Poetry was an underlying influence in father's life. It rubbed on to me early in life as he would at times read out English poems. His favourite was 'If' by Rudyard Kipling. He would become a little emotional while reciting the lines, 'Or watch the things you gave your life to, broken, and stoop and build them up with worn out tools'.

While he never spoke about the partition and bloodshed of 1947, it was clear that the suffering, tragedy and loss of Hindu–Muslim brotherhood affected him deeply. To him the poem was a combination of the basics of the goodness of all religions—a universal truth of all time. 'If' became an ode to the love between a father and a son. On joining the National Defence Academy (NDA), coincidentally, a copy of the poem appeared as my guiding star once again. Each cabin had a framed copy of the poem on the wall opposite the study table to guide the cadets to live life king-size by adhering to the guidance therein. At NDA, as well as later in life, numerous challenges would surface, but the ability and determination to overcome it all came gradually by reading poems again and again, poems that provided maturity, wisdom and inspiration.

I vividly recall a remarkable incident from my childhood, an outcome of my own mischief, which led my mother to bash me for the first time. On a lazy afternoon, Shamsher (Shammi), my elder brother, and I were experimenting with a toy string telephone. The excitement and novelty of hearing whispers travel across a considerable distance and remain audible encouraged us to increase the inter se distance. While he stood on the veranda, I walked up to the first floor to lower the string telephone. The lightweight cardboard cone was tied to the string, which served as the speaker and could not be lowered as it swayed in the breeze. To lower the speaker, I tied a jagged stone and lowered the same only to realize that the string was not long enough to reach the ground floor. I lowered myself onto the parapet to swing the string like a pendulum for Shammi to catch. Each movement added momentum to the swinging stone, which finally caught Shammi smack across his forehead. The sound of Shammi crying loudly sprang from the floor below. Before I could reach the veranda, my mother was already there, nursing his now bloodied forehead. My sudden presence was confirmation for my mother to help solve the riddle of Shammi's injury. The wound left a permanent mark on his forehead which Shamsher would subsequently proclaim as his 'third eye', an identification mark gifted by his brother. That was the first time I learnt that despite their soft and gentle demeanour, mothers possessed the muscle power to exert mercilessly when their firstborn was harmed.

In 1950 my father was posted to Allahabad—a large military cantonment and the main pay and account office for military pensions. We had a sprawling house close to the river Ganga. Soon after our arrival, one of the luminaries of India's freedom movement, Sardar Vallabhbhai Patel had passed away and a national holiday had been declared. In keeping with Hindu tradition, his ashes were to be immersed in the holy water of Ganga. The local administration had turned this into a major event; it was the final tribute to one of the most loved sons of India. I can recall thousands of people walking past our house, leading to the ghats. My parents must have greatly admired the national leader, since the whole family travelled to Draupadi Ghat in the city to pay tribute to the departed soul. As a young girl, my mother had participated in protest marches organized by the Congress in Rawalpindi, demanding freedom. The thrill of seeing an aircraft scattering rose petals over the Sangam (Triveni), the confluence of the three rivers, while we paid floral tributes sitting in a boat, is vivid in my memory. Hundreds of colourful boats floating on water, loud announcements by the police interspersed with patriotic songs blaring from the speakers leant the whole ceremony the look of a large mela.

In 1952 we had moved to Jabalpur after my father was promoted as the Deputy Controller of Defence Accounts. One of the first things he did was to enrol us in a local school. I was admitted to St. Mary's Convent School. He accompanied me on the first day, carrying some fruit and sweets to distribute among the teachers. This was an old practice in pre-partition Punjab, but it was accepted with some reservation in this school.

I had inadvertently gained notoriety a few days after joining the kindergarten class. I had joined a group of boys playing football during recess. The game continued till it started drizzling, when suddenly the boys returned to their classroom. I was the odd one out as I unwittingly kept playing football with a class that had a free period after recess. A very sheepish, hesitant, young footballer was soon escorted to his classroom, much to the merriment of all, as the teacher admonished me for my dishevelled dress and late arrival. The dressing down I received from my class teacher was communicated to Gangadhar, our help, who had come to escort us back to the house. Gangadhar gleefully reported this incident to mother to sully my reputation, branding me as naughty and carefree for a lifetime.

Between the house and the main road leading to the school, ran a parallel *kuccha* track, which was used by the bullock carts. The track went past our house and two churches with large compounds. Every morning the bullock carts would carry their wares, mostly hay, to the marketplace close by. During winter mornings, the tinkling sound of bells tied around the necks of the bullocks would announce the arrival of the convoy before dawn. Having observed it for a few days, we knew that the driver in the lead cart was always alert while those following in the carts behind would simply follow the leader in slumber. Each cart had a hurricane lamp underslung to guide the cart behind. The carts carried bundles of hay, weighing around 20 kilograms each. While we had no use for the hay, the thrill of unloading stacks of hay from moving carts needed great dexterity and sound planning, as there was no way of knowing which driver was alert. It was thrilling to be able to outwit the drivers, as the haystacks were generally well-secured, and our success rate was not always encouraging. Securing a full bundle was rare as it involved unloading and quickly moving it away from the track to hide it, while the convoy reached the track bend and went out of sight. When tired of this adventure, we would saunter across to the church close by to pluck berries or cross the road to inspect the new post and telegraph office, which was under construction at the time. Our early morning adventures continued for a few days till one of the more vigilant drivers chased us, unfortunately ending our escapade.

During the holidays or on Sunday mornings, my father would take great pleasure in cooking meat for the family. He had a unique recipe, which included adding some gram dal, a slice of turnip and some select spices to produce a mouth-watering dish to be washed down with lassi and tandoori roti. On special occasions, my mother would prepare sweetmeats and puddings laced with dry fruits or ice cream. During winter, an abundance of dry fruits would be available in jars and even lined our pockets every time we stepped out of the house. Her special preparation was *pinni* and *matthi*, served with evening tea. On some afternoons, my father would ask one Mr Chugh, working as his staff, to join in for tea and also help him with the preparation of the *janam kundlis* (birth charts) of all the children. He had documented the exact date and time of birth of each child and had forecast their future. Many of his predictions had turned out right. His forecast for himself had read, 'The 53rd will be a critical year.' He was born in 1900.

By then the family had grown to include my brothers, Rajinder, Narinder and Surinder. In mid-November 1953, my father was to conduct the final tour of all military stations under his charge across India's Eastern Sector. My mother was extremely nervous about this tour as Narinder's sporadic bouts of epilepsy were a cause of concern. After dinner, I heard father explaining to her, 'This tour is important. Very soon I am likely to be posted and promoted, maybe before the year ends.' He tried to cheer her up, but the decision to complete the tour remained unchanged despite mother's tears and pleading.

I recall his departure from home. It was a pitch-dark November night. The only light visible was that of the post and telegraph office building, still under construction across the road. One could hear from a distance, the church bell announcing that it was 2100 hours. A junior officer who was to escort father was already at the gate. As the car door opened, father patted my cheek, 'You are the brave one; look after your mother.' He had barely stepped out onto the veranda when the howling of the jackals followed by the screams of hyenas interspersed with the barking of dogs. The cantonment area was generally a desolate place with wilderness all around. Mother believed the howling of animals was bad omen. Her superstitions set in a wave of emotional distress, which was not unusual. I could sense her anxiety and deep concern. As father stepped out towards the car that awaited him, I remember mother raising her hand, as if to recall him, but stopped short suddenly, giving in to another age-old superstition, '*Janewale ko pichhe se kabhi awaz nahi dete.*' (It is not good omen to interrupt someone on their way.) Gangadhar stood close by in stoic silence.

The tour was a critical period for the family, lasting a fortnight.

As children we could sense the tension that had possessed mother. We would return from school to find her nursing Narinder or engaging in animated discussions with the neighbours. Sitting at the round dinner table, she told us that the next day she would accompany a neighbour to take Narinder to Maharishi Mahesh Yogi, who had only recently come down from the Himalayas and had a reputation for performing miracles.

We returned from school the next day to find mother extremely tense, low in spirits and highly agitated. This was perhaps the first time when steaming hot food was not already laid out on the table. Gangadhar was not at his usual place either. He had probably been sent out to procure some medicine. We tried persuading her to tell us what had happened. Unmoved, she didn't give in until Shamsher put his arms around her. She broke down at this gesture and between sobs, she narrated that as she was about to cross the threshold of the hall to meet the Maharishi, his loud voice had stopped her in her tracks. In a visibly serious voice, Maharishi Mahesh Yogi had announced, '*Rukk jaao. Aage mat aao. Tumhare kandhe par kalle badal mandra rahein hain. Tumahare jeevan mein bahut bada sankat aane wala hai.*' (Stop. Do not proceed further. Some great tragedy will occur in your life.) On hearing this, mother could not contain her emotions and started crying loudly. The lady who had accompanied her tried to console her and mentioned to the Maharishi that the lady in distress had brought her son Narinder along, as he suffered repeated bouts of *mirgi* (epilepsy). On hearing this, the Maharishi met mother and offered some ash and advised her about Narinder, '*Iska mundan kara do, theek ho jaayega.*' (Have his head shaved; he will be alright.) Then, in a more consolatory tone, he added, '*Shaant ho jaao. Himmat se kaam lo. Himmat rakho, sab theek ho jaayega.*' (Stay calm, have faith! Good days will follow soon.) She returned home, heartbroken, desolate and nervous, her whole world suddenly distorted and distressed. Having put Narinder to sleep, she entered her bedroom to receive an even bigger shock. The corner of her bedroom, which she used for routine prayers, had a bracket fitted on which stood a brass idol of Lord Hanuman, the deity she offered prayers to. She switched on the lights only to realize that the idol was not in its usual place, but had fallen off the shelf and was lying on the carpet below. This sent a tremor down her spine. She recalled her short prayer before leaving the room to visit Maharishi Mahesh Yogi. She had locked all the doors and windows and had switched off the fan. She wondered how that could have happened in a closed room that no one could possibly enter. Surely it was linked to the prophecy of the lingering dark clouds and the tragedy that Maharishi Mahesh Yogi had mentioned earlier that day. Thinking about what might be in store for herself and her family made her tremble.

Despite a sleepless night, she was up early to make sure our tiffins were ready, the school uniforms ironed and to see us off to school. She would not let the dark clouds descend on her family as was evident from her demeanour. Yet, I know that she was sitting upon a mountain of sorrow—smiling, hiding the fear, turmoil and pain within. This carried on for two, or maybe, three days. The office, meanwhile, reported that they had received word from father that the tour was going as per plan and that he would return with gifts for children.

After dinner, we were tucked into bed early as the temperature had dropped due to a cool wind blowing in the evening. As was the practice, Gangadhar had locked the doors and handed over the keys. I could hear the pitter-patter of raindrops outside and the sound of branches swaying with the increasing velocity of winds. I must have dozed off while watching my mother tossing and turning in bed alongside. In the stillness of the night, the doorbell rang and suddenly all hell broke loose. Mother sprang out of bed, possessed by some dreadful fear of danger that the ringing bell seemed to signify. After a pause, the bell rang again, a little longer as though the messenger was confirming an urgency to communicate. By now, mother had not only switched on the lights in the bedroom, but also the dining and drawing rooms. I jumped out of bed and joined her. Her trembling hands reached out to hold my hand as she called out loudly, '*Kaun hai itni raat mein jo bell baja raha hai?*' (Who is it at this odd hour?) Though loud and clear, I could sense from the tenor of her voice a strange blend of audacity laced with impending fear. The response came in a solemn voice but was terrifying in its implication, '*Mein sahib ke office se aaya hoon.* Telegram *hai.*' (I am from Sir's office and bring a telegram for you.) The sound of the word 'telegram' and 'office' electrified the environment. In those days 'telegram' implied either celebration of life or news of death and disaster. The midnight knock, the tone and timing were enough to trigger the foreboding thoughts. She shrieked at Gangadhar to come quickly and accost this unwelcome messenger, falsely claiming delivery of telegram to scare her. Gangadhar responded promptly, saying he was already near the door. A brief silence followed. As the veranda lights were switched on by Gangadhar, he started howling, shouting gibberish. Mother thought that Gangadhar had been assaulted, and in one swift movement flung the drawing room door wide open. The messenger stood right in front of her. He appeared unusually tall, wearing a grey full sleeve raincoat and a wide-brimmed hat, fully drenched, water dripping down his tall frame and raincoat, his head slightly bowed. He stood over a puddle of water, holding out a telegram in his hand. His silhouette was visible against the torrential winter rain and sharp streaks of lightning leaping up in the sky. His presence left us in no doubt that a tragedy had struck. Even before opening the telegram, mother asked Gangadhar to get up and stop crying, before she herself burst into a thunderous scream, the magnitude of which paled the lightning and thunder of the gods above.

Death had occurred at the first-class waiting room at about 2030 hours at Katihar Railway Station on 1 December 1953. It was later learnt that after completing official work at the Bihar Regimental Centre at Danapur (near Patna), my father was travelling towards Guwahati by train when he fell sick. His personal assistant (PA), a South Indian, was asked to fetch a doctor when the train halted at Katihar. When the PA did not return with the railway doctor within a reasonable time, father detrained and walked to the waiting room some distance away. He sat down on one of those old-fashioned chairs with swing arms in the railway waiting room and raised his tired feet to relax. Soon thereafter, he felt the need to wipe away the sweat from his brow. As he pulled out his red silk handkerchief from the top jacket pocket, it slipped through his fingers. The doctor arrived soon after to declare that he had died due to a heart attack. His walk had probably proved to be fatal. The PA must have sent the telegram and thereafter mysteriously disappeared, never to return to meet the family or rejoin duty.

Death can destroy families. This one was no different. My mother, a widow at 35 was saddled with five sons and a daughter, with the eldest aged around nine and the youngest barely a year old. Despite being strong, it was as if destiny had intended to test my mother's resolve to turn her suffering into what would be a life of endurance and human achievement. Her aged parents and brothers were quick to respond and arrived soon after to help her tide over the more immediate problems. This incident made her realize that the ability to read people is a critical survival skill. The greatest power you could have in life is not resources or skills but your ability to read people like a book. Given this knowledge one could distinguish friend from foe, smoking out the snakes in the grass. Her faith that Krishan, my father's younger brother, would attend the funeral and offer to help, disappointed her. Krishan had received support, shelter and financial help while struggling to complete his education and qualify as a professor and barrister. In fact, my father had always been confident that this brother would support his family if ever needed. However, the fact that Krishan did not even attend the cremation of his elder brother shattered my mother's faith. As children, we were soon to witness the radical change that consumed her; her transformation from a young dependent widow who grew in stature while complying with the crushing traditional rituals of death surprised us. Deep down she was simultaneously steeling herself to overcome grief and devote her life to a single mission of giving her children the best of what was yet to come. Her transformation and ability to accept suffering and make sacrifices can only be described best in Nietzsche's words: 'He who has a why to live for can almost bear any how.' The 'why' was to ensure her children's health, education and character and the 'how' was about learning to manage and overcome all odds. She lived up to this Nietzschean aphorism till her last breath.

One ritual that remains embedded in my mind was the 13th day ceremony after my father's death. It was held on the lawns of our Jabalpur house when relatives and friends of the family from the pre-partition days, the office staff from Indian Defence Accounts Service (IDAS) and others congregated for the condolence ceremony. While the men congregated to condole with a calm dignified silence, broken only with words of philosophical wisdom, the women would sit in a group with their face covered with a *palla*, with which they dabbed their eyes and blew their noses as they cried and wailed. This gruesome spectacle was called the *siyapa* in which the women would partially bare their breasts, their cheeks, their forehead and thighs rhythmically. To express their sympathy, each one would walk up to mother and put her hands on her shoulder and cry in an intimate language and tone. They never gave relief to the bereaved lady, who was already in deep distress. A scaled-down version of this would continue to be repeated weeks after the death every time a distant relation dropped by to condole. The sight of the women mourning was indeed depressing.

Cut off without any support from her husband's family, she chose to resettle in Lucknow. The decision was based on the pragmatic considerations of being close to her elder brother and parents while living in an independent house. Within those early months after father's demise, she had turned a new leaf and now took on the mantle that had been thrust upon her—of playing the role of an indulgent mother and an authoritarian father. A measly pension of ₹150 per month and limited savings did not deter her from doing the best for us. Having passed her matriculation from the Mission School in Rawalpindi, she took her two elder sons to La Martiniere School, but changed her mind quickly when she realized the danger of the Gomti river flowing close by. The next day she met Father Alfred, the Principal of St Francis School for the admission of her two sons and her daughter, Kusum, to the nursery class. Once their admissions were confirmed, she appealed to the principal of this Roman Catholic school that the concession being granted to Christians should be extended to non-Christian children of widows alike. Her determined appeal paved way not only for the two elder boys but all other brothers to follow in subsequent years too. After nursery, Kusum was admitted to the famed Loreto Convent as a day scholar on full fees. Mother had already made up her mind to give Kusum not only the best education but to encourage her to take up a profession as well. As a young girl, she was determined to get into higher education herself, but her parents had chosen to push her into wedlock. She would now live that dream by carefully guiding her daughter. Within a few months, after taking stock of the finances, she announced that the boys would receive education till Senior Cambridge, after which they would need to earn a living, while the daughter could pursue her dream of a chosen profession.

2

Cadet to Captain

National Defence Academy

In June 1958, my elder brother, Shamsher qualified for the National Defence Academy (NDA), Khadakwasla, Pune. This became my motivation and inspiration to qualify as well. Instead of sitting for the Senior Cambridge exam, I volunteered to write the High School examination, the minimum prerequisite for joining the NDA. The exam was considered comparatively easier and suited my academic profile, but my overconfidence led to a big jolt when the results were declared. While I had done reasonably well in all subjects, my performance in Hindi was borderline. I shared my nervousness with my siblings but maintained that I would still get the minimum passing mark of 33 per cent. However, my name did not appear in the list of students declared successful when the results were announced. The candidates who had scored between 28–33 marks in any subject would be called for re-examination and were added to a compartmental list. While my mother was disappointed, she held her cool on my assurance. The week-long wait for the marksheet was spent in sheer agony even while I kept my chin up. My siblings did their best to cheer me up, but I sought security in seclusion. The marksheet revealed that I had done well in all subjects except Hindi, in which I had scored 28 marks, the bare minimum to qualify for the compartmental test. The test was conducted after six weeks, and the results were announced another four agonizing weeks later. The Union Public Service Commission results for NDA brought some relief as I had qualified. This was followed by the Services Selection Board interview, which placed me high up on the merit list to join the NDA in January 1962.

During the second term, I broke the tibia fibula bone of my left leg while playing football and landed up in the sick bay, cast in plaster of Paris for 12 weeks. During this period, an epidemic broke out in the Academy, resulting in me being shunted to the isolation ward, along with another cadet. It was during this period that the war with China had begun. With no radio or transistor, our only source of information was the nursing orderly, who brought our regular supply of meals and tales of Indian troops being massacred. Then, one day at breakfast, he announced that Brigadier Hoshiar Singh, the Deputy Commandant, NDA had been posted out to command a brigade. That evening was special and remains embedded in my memory just as the thunderous applause and ear-splitting cry 'Brigadier Hoshiar *ki jai*' hailing the officer reverberated from the Academy auditorium to the isolation ward over 2 kilometres away. That sound still rings in my ears. It expressed the anger and disappointment of a new generation of Indians growing up with the belief of '*Hindi-Cheeni bhai bhai*'. By the time the Academy closed for the term break, the war was over, and Brigadier Hoshiar Singh was no more. I was thus deeply saddened. With my plastered leg, I proceeded on term leave for Lucknow to learn from the newspapers, radio and friends about the humiliating defeat that we had suffered and the shame that the Chinese had cast on a nascent nation. I visited the military hospital and met many of the wounded to hear their tales of defeat and the death of comrades. Dejected and saddened, I set out in search of my school friend, Ching Kong, the son of a prominent dentist. It would be the last time we would meet.

I returned home to meet a smart, debonair Shamsher, decked in his cavalry uniform and black beret, surrounded by our siblings and a proud mother, admiring the single pip on his shoulder. His training at the Indian Military Academy (IMA) had been reduced by six months due to the Indo-China War, resulting in Parchment Commission at the age of 18 years and six months. A small prayer, followed by a thanksgiving function, was organized by our united family, under the watchful eye of a favourite uncle at 9B, Hope Road, Lucknow. It signified a return to happy times. The other siblings would travel down the same path, with the spirit of hope in their hearts and the blessings of our mother, to fulfil our dearest father's last wish—that his sons must join the Defence Forces. His close interaction with the Defence officers as Deputy CDA had convinced him about their patriotism and honesty.[1]

In the NDA, cadets who drop out of their original batch on academic, medical or disciplinary grounds win the sobriquet of 'one-/two-star generals'. My three-month-long stint at the hospital, nursing a broken tibia fibula led to my relegation in the second term. I lost a term but won a star. I was dubbed a 'one-star general'. However, in my class stood a senior general with a 'two-star ranking', who outranked me with his notoriety! We were both backbenchers, and our star rating singled us out from the majority. He was physically among the toughest cadets—stout, well built with a vice-like grip and a firm handshake. On our first meeting, I placed him in the

[1] Brigadier B. S. Mehta. *The Burning Chaffees : A Soldier's First-Hand Account of the 1971 War.* Penguin, India (2021).

'strong and silent category' of people who would not suffer fools nor make unnecessary compromises to gain favours or win friendships. The backbench provided him the comfort of reading and reflecting on his inner thoughts. For me it was an escape from the drudgery of the classroom and an opportunity to interact with this person, who I prefer to identify as K2, as he wishes to remain incognito.

I was strong, well-built, athletic, a cross-country runner and a merit-card holder. However, every time we tried to test our strength in *punja* (fist fight), I would put up a stiff resistance, but finally lose to his vice-like grip and steely wrist. He would then explain his regimen, the technique and the need for regular practice to achieve invincibility in *punja*. Gradually, the dialogue shifted to books and classics. While cadets were mostly immersed in reading bestsellers by Harold Robbins, he would go for books like the thought-provoking *Atlas Shrugged* by Ayn Rand or classics such as *Brothers Karamazov* by Fyodor Dostoevsky. He would read with great intensity and even try to imbibe the values of fictional heroes. Little did I know that he would become my mentor in the world of literature and poetry.

As our friendship grew, he shared with me his knowledge of Omar Khayyam, whose works he had memorized completely. I could recall a few stanzas, but his recollection and analysis impressed me immensely. It was much later when he told me that his family used to run the popular Cheap John Store in Lahore before they had migrated to Mumbai. Both of us had applied for commission into the Armoured Corps. His battalion commander, an Armoured Corps officer, Brigadier I. S. Dhillon, had assured him that he would be assigned Hodson's Horse. Fate played foul to push him into the infantry. Disappointed, he left within a couple of years to join his father's business. How he extricated himself from military service within a short span is a remarkable story of single-mindedness and determination to reach his goal. For a young officer, circumventing a minefield of rules and regulations to achieve his singular aim makes his story remarkable, unique and worthy of being made into a film someday. His life since is in many ways a reflection of the poem 'If'—he has met 'Triumph and Disaster', 'walked with kings' but has still not lost 'the common touch'. As mentioned in Omar Khayyam's *Rubaiyat*, 'The moving finger writes and having writ, moves on ...' His struggle and success reflect his determination while the rest of us kept soldiering on!

Adjusting to the NDA regimen was an uphill task. A cadet's life was busy—one never had time 'to stand and stare'. It provided no time to ponder over one's difficulties, one just went ahead and did what was required. The days passed in a haze of perpetual fatigue. We were always racing against time. This cradle of leadership transformed cadets from boys to men. It taught us to cope with adversity. It stretched us to the limits that we never knew existed. The training moulded our overall personality, while all the sports that we played instilled team spirit in us. We learnt not only about the defence services, but also how to deal with people and tackle the challenges that life posed.

I graduated from the NDA in June 1965 to report to the Indian Military Academy (IMA) at Dehradun. I had been assigned to Alamein Company. The major change was our newfound status of Gentlemen Cadets. The IMA laid greater stress on military training and the duties of platoon commanders or equivalent in military units. The cadets of 28 NDA and 37 IMA earned their first pip on 15 June 1966, after an impressive passing out parade held at the IMA grounds. I would, in due course, receive my Parchment Commission signed by the President of India, Dr S. Radhakrishnan. I had been assigned to 45 Cavalry.

Bagrakote

Within a few days of joining 45 Cavalry at Babina in July 1966, my regiment moved to Bagrakote, West Bengal. Bagrakote is at the northern tip of the strategic narrow Siliguri corridor, which links the Northeastern states to the rest of India. The excitement of guarding the critical Siliguri corridor evaporated as we battled mosquitoes, leeches and humidity. Bagrakote was devoid of basic infrastructure and amenities including electricity. The exquisite flora and fauna and awe-inspiring sunsets over the tea gardens were wasted on us as we struggled inside a dormitory, consisting of a bamboo hut, with a thatched roof and rusted, corrugated iron sheets, a dilapidated common bathroom devoid of piped water and a flush toilet. A few temporary huts built by the Military Engineer Service and *bashas*[2] constructed by the previous unit out of their funds to meet local needs were all that was available. There were no garages for the tanks or vehicles. A small detachment of Military Engineer Services, forming part of a Station HQ, was located at New Mal, a railhead about 25 kilometres away. The unit, carrying crores worth of battleworthy equipment, that was sensitive to the vagaries of the weather, had been inducted into a field area without due thought about infrastructure and amenities. This was the harsh reality of military existence. Babina was indeed a trailer that got to suck you into this neglected corridor, now renamed as Buggerkote.

When the going gets tough, the tough get going. During one's early life, school and later while training at the Academy, one had accepted this dictum as a universal truth. The collective effort of the officers and men transformed the environment within a few weeks to make the unit area habitable. Junior commissioned officers (JCOs) invoked the beg, borrow and steal approach, while the officers put their heads together to exploit contacts and ex-regimental officers for the release of tents, tarpaulins, stores and funds. A stoic silence and a cheerful demeanour helped us to overcome organizational failures. Initiative, innovation, trust and faith were no longer catchwords

---

[2] A thatched hut; improved versions of a *basha* had an asbestos roofng

but operating systems. Difficulties encouraged bonding and eased personal communication. Accepting responsibility to make one's troops and oneself comfortable was an early lesson that we had learnt. Before long, we were able to invite commanders of local formations and managers of neighbouring tea gardens to our modified officers' mess. Socializing with the local tea planters, cricket and golf matches, visits to Siliguri for books, magazines and purchase of transistors, sports goods, among others, broke the monotony. Some of the more adventurous also ventured into the border town of Dhulabari to buy smuggled imported goods from Indian traders operating from Nepal.

The conduct of senior officers posted to this new raising made one realize that loyalty to one's regiment was a lifelong commitment. In those days, getting posted out of one's regiment to a new raising was viewed as a punishment. The bonds formed were so strong that officers were often ready to sacrifice their careers and forgo promotions. The record of officers posted to 45 Cavalry was no different. Some found their way back to their original regiments or other regiments holding similar equipment. The other reason that contributed to the exodus was the PT-76 tank itself. This was a light, amphibious tank, shaped like a boat, with a 76-millimetre gun. It was considered a poor cousin of other tanks that were in use. Additionally, the 45 Cavalry was raised on the organization of a light regiment. While standard regiments had 14 tanks per squadron, split into four tank troops of three tanks each and two at the Station HQ, this light regiment had three tank troops of three tanks and two at the Station HQ. In addition, the light regiment was authorised two rifle troops, each equipped and trained to carry out operations like the integral infantry of the regiment. The role and modus operandi of the Light Cavalry Regiment was repulsive to the hardcore officers of Armoured Corps coming from the armoured division. During the 1965 war, the PT-76 was deployed in the Western Sector by 7 Light Cavalry. It had gained notoriety due to its poor performance in the battlefield. After the war ended, their tanks were transferred to 45 Cavalry. Those coming from Centurion regiments scoffed at the PT-76 and expressed it as unworthy for a tank versus tank battle. The others who stayed on fell into two categories—some who willingly accepted the change while others who realized that they were surplus to their previous regiments. Those commissioned directly into 45 Cavalry would become hardcore officers, who would bring repute to the regiment in the future.

The Army List of 1970 recorded my name under 45 Cavalry as Substantive Lieutenant/Acting Captain B. S. Mehta, date of commission: 15 June 1966, date of birth: 16 April 1945. I mostly served in the Eastern Sector for the first five years. I had served in two SIC (South Indian Classes) squadrons and the OIC (Other Indian Classes) squadron. The OICs were denied combat service, having been branded non-martial by the British. During this period, I had held all staff appointments at the regimental level. I had completed the compulsory military examinations and attended professional courses, including the Commando Course at the Infantry School at Mhow and the Short Staff Course at Shillong, under Colonel K. Sundarji (later COAS). I had read reports and books on the partition and military operations undertaken by our Army post-independence. The mind stood conditioned to stories one had heard from elders sitting around the family fireplace, describing eyewitness accounts of murder and mayhem during the partition in 1947, my own recollection of the NDA and IMA days and the stories of valour and glory of serving and retired officers and *jawans*. The elan and panache of the cavalry were inbuilt in one's DNA and reinforced by the experiences one had lived through during service. While it did not make one a warmonger or create a pathological hatred for any class or community, it was evident that I would rejoin my regiment if ever a shooting war was announced. The popular two-liner, which was often-repeated by both my parents, had reinforced this inclination during our growing up years—'*Girte hain shah sawaar hi maidan-e-jung mein, woh tifleh kya gire jo guthnoh ke bal chale.*' (Only the brave who ride high in the battlefield run the risk of failing, for what can the pygmies who know none else but to crawl ever hope to gain.) I suspect others of my generation, exposed to similar influences, would also be swayed likewise.

As a family, my mother's dream stood nearly accomplished. Rajinder, my younger brother, had been commissioned into 16 Light Cavalry. Narinder had joined the NDA in 1968 and had earned his Parchment Commission in November 1971 to join 5 GARHWAL[3]. The youngest, Surinder, had completed the Senior Cambridge examination with a first division from St Francis and was awaiting his interview call from the Services Selection Board. Kusum, our only sister, had appeared for the pre-medical test and cleared her admission into King George Medical College, Lucknow in the Dentistry Department. Mother had devoted her life to her children despite all odds, fighting a mountain of difficulties that a widow must face in society. On the days when she would be in a pensive mood, she would recall Ghalib's couplet, '*Ranj se khugar hua insaan to mit jata hai ranj, mushkilein mujh par padi itni ke aasaan ho gayi.*' (When one experiences extreme grief and suffering in life, one becomes so accustomed to it that even grief ceases to be.) The courage and character she displayed during those challenging years gave her a new iconic status within the family, friends and in the neighbourhood.

Kanchrapara

Having spent nearly five years at Bagrakote, the regiment was moved to a peace station—Ramgarh, near Ranchi (Jharkhand). This

[3] 5th Regiment, The Garhwal Rifles

turned out to be a brief interlude, as within months, the unit was called out for aid to civil authority and deployed in Kanchrapara, near Barrackpore. Elections had been announced in West Bengal, where the Communist Party of India and Congress were the main contenders. The law and order problems were challenged by the large spread of Naxalites across the state. The regiment deployed about three columns to carry out flag marches and ensure free and fair polls. This allowed us to get a feel of the district level administration and to meet the *babu, bhondu, bania and badmash*, all of whom were well spread out in the district and controlling the countryside. The duties as column commander included conducting flag marches, which was generally detested by both the troops as well as the officers. The general apathy and neglect of the civil administration and the functioning of the cogs in the wheels of district authorities and police left one disillusioned.

The regimental officers spent a memorable Christmas and New Year in the famed clubs of Calcutta, dancing till the wee hours to the live bands playing songs of the Beatles and Boney M. The bonhomie did not last long. We had barely stepped into the New Year when the developments in the neighbourhood shattered the hopes of our return to the peace station.

The year 1971 was significant for South Asia. In India, Indira Gandhi had been elected to the office of Prime Minister with a commanding parliamentary majority. In Pakistan, General Yahya Khan had held the first national election based on universal adult franchise that would divide the country instead of uniting it. Before the end of the year, two wars had been fought in Pakistan, one internally and the other with India. The first led to millions of refugees, mostly Hindus from East Pakistan, seeking refuge in the economically impoverished Indian states in the east.

The unit was mobilized due developments in East Pakistan. Ramgarh was no longer a peace station but became the rear location for the unit where families continued to reside while the unit got deployed under 9 Infantry Division on the border. As young officers, we were witnessing the transition from leading flag marches through the crowded streets of West Bengal to leading tank troops and mobilization drills and recce along with infantry units. It was tougher for the married officers and *jawans* who, while performing military duties, had one eye fixed on the regimental rear for maintenance and the other on the upkeep of their families and children. That so many of us in uniform would have to sacrifice such long hours of our youthful lives preparing for a war that had not even been sounded, is the stuff that army life is made up of. The citizen remains ignorant and lacks the experience to appreciate that blood and sweat in peace alone can bring victory in war. The citizen mistakenly believes that their approbation or cash contribution equates their patriotism with that of a soldier's. It is this uninitiated class of citizens that bays for the enemy's blood to fulfil some hidden agenda and arouse the less educated to join the national upsurge. Soldiering is not a world cup match where you shake hands or tear shirts. It is a more serious business where you determine the destiny of nations. The soldier returns from the battlefield to his home and hearth, unhonoured and unsung, to start again at the beginning, without breathing a word about his loss. Neither the government nor society can ever give him enough to compensate for the precious moments of his life spent preparing for war—not his war—our war, our freedom, our destiny and the nation's destiny.

Operation Searchlight

By the late 1960s, West Pakistan had done everything to create animosity with its Eastern side. Their problems were not limited to physical separation, language, and trust alone, but were in fact deep-rooted. The popular joke was that the two wings were united by three things: Islam, English and Pakistan International Airlines. The disparate representation of Bengalis in the armed forces and civil services only added to the alienation. Politically, the Six-point Programme of Awami League's Sheikh Mujibur Rahman had been rejected by the military leadership of West Pakistan in 1966. To add to their woes, an extremely severe cyclonic storm, called Bhola, struck on 11 November 1970, devastating East Pakistan (and India's West Bengal). An absolute disregard on the government's part converted this crisis into a mass movement, with the people demanding a breakaway from the ruling junta. Meanwhile, the elections held on 7 December 1970 gave an overwhelming majority to the Awami League, which sent shivers to the ruling junta. Attempts for a compromise between the Awami League and Bhutto's Pakistan People's Party were jettisoned after Bhutto's infamous speech *'Idhar hum, udhar tum'*. Bhutto was supported by the military leadership under Yahya Khan. Martial law was declared, and General Tikka Khan was appointed as the governor and brought in to crush the Bengali nationalistic movement. With this objective in mind, a planned military operation called Operation Searchlight was conducted by the Pakistan Army by taking control over the major cities on 25 March 1971. It was a military solution to a political problem that finally led to genocide, rape and plunder by the Pakistan Army. The large-scale influx of refugees into India became an unacceptable threat to the security and domestic tranquillity of India's Eastern and Northeastern states. The suffering of the refugees had galvanized our nation on humanitarian grounds. India had upheld its traditional values by keeping its borders open for refugees to enter and return at will. The imposition of refugee tax, to share the burden of maintenance with Indian citizens, reflected our deep concern for their well-being. The support provided to the Bangladesh government-in-exile and training to the Mukti Bahini strengthened their resolve to undertake this fight for liberation in conjunction with the Indian Army. The Pakistani decision makers did not visualize the probability of war when they unleashed Operation Searchlight. They were satisfied that the traitors and miscreants, along with other Hindu refugees, had either fled or been dispersed. The onset of monsoon created hope that stability and order had been restored by the military in East Pakistan.

The thought of war in April or May was considered improbable. The picture changed during August, September and October due to the activities of Mukti Bahini, with tacit support and training from India, making war a probability that could be avoided. This was in sync with the commonly shared perception of the Pakistani governing elite that the international community would constrain any Indian propensity for aggression, and that if hostilities did commence, it would be halted before Indian victory, as had been the pattern of the three wars that were fought earlier during the first 25 years of independence.

Ahmednagar

My posting to Ahmednagar did not come as a surprise as many of my batchmates were being posted out from units on to their first Extra Regimental Employment (ERE). The ERE ensured all-round professional growth of officers, exposing them to different military and staff duties. Having completed an extended temporary duty tenure for the installation of a tankodrome (tactical training complex), it was expected that I would be posted to maintain and run the newly commissioned unit of the gunnery wing.

During mid-1971, there were rumours that the refugee problem would continue unabated and that Pakistan was not inclined to take them back. India's appeal to the international community brought some sympathy and limited relief. The military establishment read the signs correctly and had begun to set its own house in order and prepare for the contingency of war. Within the Indian defence establishment, the general feeling was that the 1962 war was a wake-up call for the nation. It shook up the defence establishment, and training establishments continued to upgrade and modernize the equipment profile, which changed the outlook and thinking of the Indian Army. The 1965 war ended as a stalemate as the integration of the three services as well as the equipment profile needed an overhaul. The process of modernization was still underway in 1971. The decision to hold fast till the monsoons were over and utilize the time to prepare for the contingency of war helped. The transition found India prepared for the 1971 war. Higher defence management, civil-military relations and inter-ministry coordination with the Service Headquarters were pursued with vigour and diligence. Political direction, intelligence gathering and training of the paramilitary had received a major boost.

The first hint that India had made up its mind to resolve the crisis of millions of refugees pouring into India came with the visit of the Defence Minister Jagjivan Ram to the Armoured Corps Centre and School (ACC&S), Ahmednagar in late September 1971. He was accompanied by the senior officials of the Ministry of Defence and the HQ Southern Command. A lunch was hosted for the visiting dignitaries at the cavalry mess by Brigadier K. K. Kaul. In the welcome speech, Kaul highlighted that while tension on the borders could lead to war, the Armoured Corps was deficient in spares for tanks and ammunition. Jagjivan Ram utilized the opportunity to admonish the commandant by making a strong statement that the Army had officers to resolve problems. He then added that as defence minister, it was his responsibility to ensure that all shortcomings were made up. He then informed all present that the war would be fought not on Indian soil but enemy soil. The thunderous applause was enough to bring the roof down, sending a wave of cheer and celebration, enough to convince the visiting delegation that the Armoured Corps was itching for such an opportunity.

October is the harbinger of balmy weather in Ahmednagar. Khutub Hai (3 Cavalry) and I were finishing a round of golf when V. K. Malhotra, 17 Poona Horse, came up, waving the Military Secretary branch signal announcing the posting of the three of us—Mallu, a friend and coursemate, was to revert to his regiment, 17 Poona Horse, while Khutub Hai, my golfing companion, and I were directed to report to 80 Armoured Delivery Regiment located at Delhi Cantonment. We were placed on a seven-day notice to report to our new duty stations. Considerably deflated and demoralized at the prospect of serving in this new assignment, Khutub and I had resolved to find our way back to our regiments. As young officers, we had heard instances of how officers and men had overcome all rules and sometimes employed questionable stratagems to find their way back into their regiments. Regimental officers feel a moral obligation to be with the troops and not be left out of battle which is repugnant to soldiering; the simple soldierly motive is to live and serve with honour—death or glory are incidental.

War of Liberation

By early November, the situation had transformed itself from confrontation to a state of virtual war. In his address to the nation, on 19 November 1971, Yahya Khan had declared that Pakistan would defend its honour and territorial integrity at any cost. He had extended a hand of friendship, inviting India to grasp it and let us begin a new era of good neighbourly relations. This offer had appeared surreal to India, lacking seriousness as well as trust. The Western press was beginning to see the incongruity of

Pakistani declarations and also the plight of the 10 million refugees now residing in India. Tales of genocide and brutality by the Pakistan Army had been verified by independent organizations, resulting in empathy for the Bengali fight for independence and acknowledgement that it was a humanitarian battle for liberty and human dignity. As junior officers, we would often discuss the role of outstanding personalities like P. N. Haksar, R. N. Kao, D. P. Dhar, T. N. Kaul and K. F. Rustamji, loosely referred to as the Kashmiri mafia. K. Subrahmanyam, a strategic thinker, visionary and the director of the prominent Institute of Defence Studies and Analysis in New Delhi had developed a sterling reputation for accurate analysis. Young officers of my generation who had grown up around the time of partition carried unhappy memories of the 1962 debacle and the unfinished war of 1965. Many were now commissioned into the defence forces and had an important and glorious role to play in delivering the kick in the gut to Pakistani dignity and military pride. They were influenced by the leadership of military stalwarts like General Sam Manekshaw, Lieutenant General J. S. Aurora, Lieutenant General Sagat Singh, Lieutenant General J. F. R. Jacob and Major General Inderjit Singh Gill. Defence Minister Jagjivan Ram and Prime Minister Indira Gandhi were pillars of sagacity, statesmanship and determination. The six months of additional time for groundwork had sharpened focus and built a new level of confidence across board. J. F. R. Jacob had written to an officer saying, 'It was now the season for war—the monsoons were over, the Army had had time to train, the wintry weather in the Himalayas would foil any Chinese troops. In the East, conditions were ripe for a swift offensive.' On 18 November 1971, a cabinet meeting under Indira Gandhi had permitted Indian troops to cross the international border in self-defence to neutralize the Pakistani artillery fire that was causing loss of life and property to our civilians residing along the IB. The die was thus cast.

3

From the Battleground

Garibpur Tank versus Tank Battle

On 18 November 1971, we had moved into the forward concentration area, a few kilometres short of the international border, near Jessore Sector, East Pakistan. There was little doubt in the minds of the tank crews that war was the only alternative for resolving the crisis. The Indian history of never crossing an international border to attack or annexe another country negated this belief; some of the more seasoned seniors felt that a compromise solution would be accepted and troops would be asked to return to the barracks. They were proven wrong as the Pakistani F-86 Sabre jets could be seen crossing our airspace and carrying out strikes against our gun positions. On 20 November, the Regimental Order group (O group) had assembled for orders, while the young officers assembled near the officers' mess tent, anxious to hear the final verdict.

By midday, orders were received for 'C' Squadron to cross the international border and link up with elements of 14 PUNJAB[1]. The task set was to cut the road Chaugacha-Jessore in the vicinity of village Garibpur, about 10 kilometres from the IB by last light on 20 November. The movement across the Kabodak river presented no problem for the amphibious tanks. Troops of 14 PUNJAB rode piggy back on tanks and we were in the vicinity of the roadblock site at dusk. A hasty defence was set up by the battalion, while the tanks spread out across the infantry company locations. The general atmosphere was one of a mock annual training exercise conducted with troops and a non-existent enemy, as neither a single bullet had been fired nor any enemy activity noticed.

By midnight, the enemy movement on the Chaugacha-Jessore road created a wave of excitement. This was however short-lived as the identity of the enemy, or the equipment needed corroboration through patrols and visual observations. The preparations of setting up a hasty defence continued.

On the morning of 21 November, a dense fog covered the entire defended area, restricting visibility to a few yards. Besides the numbness of hands and ears, a sense of isolation due to limited visibility created a strange, uncomfortable feeling. It was as if one was wrapped inside a white cocoon without any visible landmarks. All thoughts of the enemy receded as the only visible activity was that of tank crews brewing tea on a bone-chilling morning. Jatin Chandra Chakraborty, the troop leader, still busy shaving, had ordered two mugs of tea for me and Lieutenant T. S. Sidhu. From the nearby trench, a tall handsome Sikh of Punjab battalion appeared carrying more tea and insisted we partake same. The conversation soon turned to the enemy activity noticed during the night. The Sikh soldier described his plight of digging a weapon pit all night as the company commander relocated the defended locality, after

[1] 14th Battalion, The Punjab Regiment

hearing from tank crews about the likely presence of enemy tanks. ' We love you but do not trust you as you change locations at short notice, leaving our defences exposed,' he remarked even under prevailing tension and hostile weather, this had the listeners in peals of laughter.

Unknown to those present, a message had been received for half the squadron to move to a different location under the squadron second-in-command. I had taken a few puffs of cigarette when a loud ear shattering explosion interrupted the friendly banter. The tank crews scampered away to mount their tanks; their worst fears confirmed. I was adjusting the neck strap of my headgear, while the gunner got busy with the gun controls when I heard snippets of a garbled message on the squadron radio net of enemy tanks advancing. The air was soon full of lead and noise, mingled with the detonation of high explosives and armour piercing shells. 'See that big one, there, get the bastard quickly.' The gunner was already aligning the gun tube in the given direction while the loader shouted, 'Loaded', followed by the terrible swoosh of the gun and recoil, the dust and fumes causing obscuration. 'I got him, Sir! Destroyed!' Even while I was complimenting the alert gunner, I could see the enemy crew bailing out as the tank had caught fire. Other tanks of the squadron gave us no chance to react as a fresh salvo blew the burning tank and crew to smithereens.

The advance of enemy tanks came to a sudden halt as 4–5 bonfires lit up the battle ground and pushed back the screen of fog. The remaining tanks would withdraw and regroup along with the infantry for a fresh attack. It was my operator, Shibe Lal, frantically trying to draw my attention to an incoming call from Colonel D. S. Jamwal (Digby), Commandant, 45 Cavalry. He appeared upset that Squadron Commander Major D. S. Narag (Chiefy) had not responded to multiple calls. Colonel Jamwal had been following the progress of the battle by listening to the transmissions on the squadron net.

He had understandably missed out on L. D. Dineshwar's message, announcing that Chiefy had been martyred. I reluctantly shared the tragic news and the circumstances under which I had to take over command of the squadron.

An extract from my book *The Burning Chaffees* describes the night of 21 November 1971 after the Tank versus Tank Battle:

The muteness of a graveyard now enveloped the battlefield, broken now and then by a salvo fired by the guns to remind us that war was still on. The muffled sound of metal striking against metal indicated that somebody was repairing his damaged tank track. I was sitting on my tank with my legs spread out in front of me and my back resting against the sloped turret. Ahead of me, in the area where the Tank v. Tank Battle had taken place, could be seen a few bonfires. These tanks were still burning bright. The wild tongues of flame had now subsided, giving way to an orange glow, which appeared brighter in the light breeze. There seemed to be a strange hypnotic charm attached to these bonfires for I felt my eyes getting transfixed on the orange and blue of the flames, forming a rich hue. I kept watching these for very long, oblivious of my surroundings. It is difficult to describe, with any degree of accuracy, the thoughts that ran through my mind then. There was a feeling of happiness and satisfaction that the enemy tanks were burning. Perhaps many of those who were killed or wounded in today's action were still lying inside. My own fate could have been no different from what I was witnessing, had the Gods in heaven not been providing a protective umbrella for me. These bonfires were the only visible reminders of the recently fought battles. My eyes moved from one bonfire to another. The smell of burning flesh mingled with that of melting iron plates and burning rubber made the atmosphere a little pungent. Amongst the many burning tanks, one at least was ours. The body of the gunner could not be recovered as the tank was in flames. This man was my responsibility and I felt disgust rising within me, trying to find some justification for the burning funeral pyre. Revulsion soon gave way to consideration, a sense of justice. Did not somebody say that all is fair in love and war? This was war. I looked back at the bonfires, for it was, after all, a beautiful sight. Thoughts, which had been freely floating around like a balloon, suddenly burst when the reality of the cigarette butt that I was holding singed my finger.

I adjusted my overcoat around my shoulders, aware of the nip in the air. The thought of death crossed my mind. I had been faced with death a number of times that day but even when I had come close to it, it eluded me. Did the hand of providence save me for another day? That it would come one day was, of course, beyond doubt. What amused me considerably was that the face of death held no special horror. Either way, it was far from all that the poets, painters and priests had made one believe, something dreadful and terrifying. The face of death in the early stages of the battle had invoked fear. This fear was no different from what one felt before entering the boxing ring. It was the fear of the unknown, which created a vacuum in the pit of your stomach, soon washed away after the first couple of blows are traded. The fear of death creates the same distressed feeling before the first few gunshots. This fear is apt to rise again, whenever the mind and body are placed in a dangerous situation. However, the mind, having reacted to it earlier, learns to accept it with more grace under pressure. So, death, once you have stared at it eyeball-to-eyeball, laughed in its very face or felt it brushing against you, creates no panic. It becomes a way of life. When I first looked down the barrel of the enemy tank, which was subsequently knocked down at a range of 30 metres, the same uneasy feeling arose in the pit of the stomach. This realization was repeated a little later, when, accompanied by my tank crew, we went charging down, to retrieve and safeguard our tank being engaged by an RCL. We were all contemplating death during that mad scramble to save our tank in the moments that followed. We were convinced that the second round from the RCL gun would destroy our tank, but we risked our lives as it had become a symbol of our pride without which life would become agonizing. Why we rushed into the jaws of death was not because a tank was more precious than our lives but because along with it, our honour and prestige would have been blown to pieces. It is in these moments of existence that the true significance of life, discipline, loyalty, pride, honour, comradeship, sacrifice and patriotism dawns on you. Based on one's individual experiences and consequent interpretations, evolves a new pattern of life. It carries within its liberal knowledge of the meaning of life and an appreciative understanding of one's fellow beings. Life, in the possible contemplation of death, then becomes more enjoyable and more rewarding![2]

Impact of the Battle of Garibpur

The Battle of Garibpur represents a significant and radical change in the political and military mindset of the country. It was on this day that the Mitro Bahini (Allied Forces) of India and Bangladesh was formalized to undertake joint operations in the War of Liberation, under the overall command of GOC-in-C (General Officer Commanding-in-Chief), Eastern Command, Lieutenant General J. S. Aurora. India's image of *ahimsa parmodharma* had radicalized into realpolitik. It was beginning to shed its historical baggage of defeat and subjugation by foreign powers. The Battle of Garibpur became synonymous with military victory and inspired not only the defence forces but the entire nation to rise as one and say with pride, '*Hum hain Hindustani!*' (We are Hindustani!) It moulded

[2] Brigadier B. S. Mehta. *The Burning Chaffees : A Soldier's First-Hand Account of the 1971 War.* Penguin, India (2021).

the nation and enthused the leadership to project the country as an assertive and responsible regional power on the subcontinent, capable of projecting its cultural identity, human values and military might. This early victory served as a trumpet call across the globe, announcing the birth of a new nation—Bangladesh. Future historians would record 21 November 1971 as the day when India transformed itself from a struggling, non-aligned Third World country, traversing world capitals with a beggar's bowl in hand, to a South Asian power and an emerging world leader.

Pakistan declared war on 3 December 1971. By the time the war ended on 16 December 1971, I had led the 'C' Squadron during the battle of Burinda, advanced to Jessore followed by a wide outflanking movement to Ramnagar. The slow advance of 9 Division, which had got bogged down along the main axis between Ramnagar and Siramani finally led to the squadron being split into penny packets. Finally, a composite half-squadron consisting of one tank troop of 'B' Squadron, with Lieutenant P. P. S. Bhandari and Lieutenant P. C. Mishra, was placed under my command to conduct a wide outflank to Khulna from the west in conjunction with HQ 42 Infantry Brigade after crossing the mighty tidal river Bhairab. When ceasefire was announced on 16 December 1971, this composite half squadron of 45 Cavalry was responding to final orders from Brigadier K. L. Kochhar, Rajputana Rifles, for opposed river crossing at Khulna.

On 16 December Lieutenant General A. A. K. Niazi surrendered to Lieutenant General J. S. Aurora, along with 93,000 prisoners of war. US President Richard Nixon and Henry Kissinger congratulated themselves for achieving their fundamental goal—the preservation of West Pakistan. Kissinger's famous last words to Nixon, while congratulating him for the ceasefire were, 'It is an absolute miracle, Mr President! We have converted disaster into defeat.'

4

Move to the Western Front

Even while the surrender ceremony was in progress, a rumour was afloat that the regiment would be de-inducted on priority as the ceasefire on the Western Front had not taken place. The same evening the officers had assembled in the field mess for drinks and dinner. Many of us were meeting after a long time. The joy and bonhomie did not last long as news of the move of the regiment to the Western Front was confirmed. The next morning tanks moved on tracks to Jessore. After a night halt, they would move back to Kanchrapara. Four special tank trains had been marshalled to carry the regiment to Suratgarh. A two-day break at Kanchrapara for rest, refit and maintenance had been arranged. The trains would move on white-hot priority, stopping only for a change of railway engine, or technical halts.

On 19 December 1971, young officers were sitting around a makeshift breakfast table, each narrating their war experiences. The commandant had called for his 'O' group to give out the schedule of the move. One of the youngsters was imitating two of Digby's favourite phrases—'Button up the loose ends', 'Pull up your socks'—

for the merriment of all. The night before the Tank versus Tank Battle, Ravi Bains, the Information Officer (IO), was narrating his discussion with me to the other officers present at the table. Most of them listened with rapt attention and in total silence. That Ravi could recall the exact conversation verbatim surprised me. While listening to him, I removed the pistol from the holster and kept it on the breakfast table in front of me. The narration was coming to an end when some more details were called for by the officers, which I gladly answered. The excitement of listening to others narrate their battle tales led to much backslapping and leg-pulling among officers. Someone cautioned Ravi not to point a gun at him, but there was no alarm, and the bonhomie continued. Ravi, forever a little careless, while toying with the gun, had inadvertently pushed the safety lever off. While saying some words of endearment, he pointed the pistol towards me and accidentally pressed the trigger. The sound of a pistol shot left everyone astonished. I do not recall the bullet, or the sound of a shot fired at me due to the proximity. All that I can recall is being shocked, stunned into silence, not being able to react to this sudden development. This state of being dumbfounded, looking at the terrified faces of those around startled me. I was no longer in control of myself. Shaken by the incident, I felt that my breath had been pulled out of my lungs. Someone was shouting at the top of his voice, cursing Ravi Bains as the bullet grazed past my temple. The tension and sudden shock made me delirious, and I burst into loud uncontrolled laughter. Poor Ravi did not know where to hide as the officers, having overcome their shock, got busy to relieve Bains from holding the pistol in his shivering hands, while some chased me around the mess tent as I moved around like a man possessed by some spirit. My wild uncontrolled ghoulish laughter and the sound of the pistol shot brought Colonel D. S. Jamwal and his 'O' group officers out to witness what must have appeared a comical sight. Fortunately, the tense moment passed with the realization that no one had sustained injuries. The hallucination phase had passed when Ravi, feeling deeply embarrassed, offered me profound apologies. This was wasted on me since I interpreted this close call as yet another experience of celebrating the gift of life; to die at the hands of a dear friend would have denied me martyrdom. I compliment myself to date on having selected a dear friend who was not a sharpshooter even at point-blank range. As it generally happens, one of the officers let sarcasm overtake his emotions and spoke unhesitatingly—'Bastard, you did not fire a single shot during the war, only to end up firing at your superior officer!'

On returning to Kanchrapara, there was time to reflect on what all had transpired in the last few weeks and catch up on the home front. On 9 December 1971, after the Battle of Ramnagar, while we had stopped at a particular bound, the Senior JCO (Junior Commissioned Officer), Raghubir Chandra handed over a telegram to me containing news of my younger brother Narinder being wounded in battle while leading a company attack of 5 GARHWAL[1] at Hilli. He was being evacuated to a command hospital. The thought that evacuation to a command hospital is for serious injuries now gripped my mind. I remembered reading the telegram in the midst of a limited operation that was underway. Instead of pocketing the telegram, the realization that I could do nothing while the battle raged had me give necessary orders on the radio for the squadron to move. The crew around me, as well as Captain Harbans Saighal, the FOO (Forward Observation Officer), was watching me intensely to gauge my reaction. Even as the radio net was beginning to buzz, I stretched my hand and tore the telegram into small pieces, with tears in my eyes and a prayer for my brother. I let the pieces fly as the tank moved on. The torn bits of the telegram fell all around the Senior JCO Raghubir, who stood below the tank. He was awestruck. He looked up in deep admiration,

[1] 5th Battalion, The Garhwal Regiment

first at me and then at the bits of paper floating overhead. He was aware of the contents of the telegram and of the impending task. He understood and appreciated my response. Soldiering demands great control over one's emotions, especially as an officer; what I had done was the only practical and responsible act expected of me. In fact, the memory of this event and the trying circumstances strengthened my resolve to visit the Command Military Hospital and meet my wounded brother. The crew and many others in the squadron had probably known the contents of the open telegram, as news of death and injury spreads by word of mouth and reached all before being delivered through mail.

Once in Kanchrapara, having visited the squadron and briefed the crew about the maintenance task, I was on the lookout for Major Surinder Singh. He was not at the maintenance parade, so I sauntered off towards the Regimental Headquarters (RHQ) to find Colonel Digby, Major P. Bhore (2IC), Major Kushal Chowdhury (OC HQ Squadron) and Major Surinder Singh—all standing together in an animated discussion. My presence interrupted their conversation, which appeared unusual. I addressed my request to Digby, 'Sir, I have to go to Calcutta to meet my younger brother Narinder, who is admitted at the Command hospital.'

Wearing a look of annoyance, Digby retorted, 'Have you asked your squadron commander?' I was stunned by his lack of empathy. Maybe he was unaware of the telegram that had been delivered to me a few days ago. What followed was a testy exchange with my superiors.

Me: 'No. He is standing here with you; he must have heard me.'

Bhore: 'Can't you see we are busy?'

Me: 'My request is addressed to the commandant, not you.'

Surinder spoke in his squeaky voice, avoiding direct confrontation.

Chowdhury: 'Balram, you go to the squadron, we will be there shortly.'

Me: 'I am coming from the squadron after briefing the crew. Since you were not there, I had to come here.'
Bhore: 'Now please leave. You have heard us all.'
Digby: 'Sorry, leave cannot be granted. You are moving with the first train tomorrow.'
Me: 'A Major joined the war seven days late due to an illness in the family. Why are you denying me permission to meet my brother who is wounded in battle? Need I say more of how the men reacted to his absence?'

I looked at Digby to gauge his response to the challenge delivered. What was Digby's compulsion to grant leave except for the fact that they had served in the same regiment together before coming to 45 Cavalry? I had taken over command of 'C' Squadron in the midst of the Tank versus Tank Battle after Major D. S. Narag was killed in action, and Lieutenant Tejinder Singh Sidhu followed by Second Lieutenant Narain Singh were wounded in action. With seven officers senior to me in the regiment and a couple of subalterns present, no one was appointed to command 'C' Squadron or troop leaders posted to assist me even while two subalterns had been attached to the Division HQ to run errands for commanders and staff. It was quite clear in my mind that Digby had made a professional compromise, bordering on dereliction of duty, and I would challenge him if push came to shove. The fire in the eye, the moral authority and conviction of my manner and speech was clearly understood by everyone, with no need for me to say more. It was amply clear that I was not going to buckle down and plead permission. Bhore and Chowdhury now stood by as silent spectators as Digby indicated through his silence that Surinder had to respond. I now placed my demand in uncompromising terms once again.

Me: 'I need a jeep to go down to Calcutta. I will be back before the

> train moves. I have to meet my brother.'
> Digby: 'Now please leave.'
> I gave Surinder a hard look. He had experienced my resolve during battle. His eyes were still avoiding mine.
> I saluted and walked away, but before leaving I added, 'Don't rush. Take your time. I know what you are doing. I am leaving now and will return before the special train leaves.'

Having said that, I walked back to the squadron, got into my jeep and drove past the RHQ mafia. I only required the sanction to travel by military transport to Calcutta. No sanctions were required by an officer to move his jeep to the Kanchrapara railway station. I returned later in the evening by the Lal Gola local shuttle.

This incident has an important bearing not because of my brush with senior officers in the regiment, but due to multiple other reasons for which the regimental mafia was responsible. The truth can never be hidden, especially in a regiment. An officer of the Division HQ on his way to Calcutta had mentioned to some regimental officers that an inquiry had been ordered against a very senior major of the regiment caught red-handed looting a watch shop in Jessore by the Divisional Field Security Section. The NCO driver of the officer had given a written statement during the interrogation. The rumours were rampant, and in most cases, the finger of suspicion pointed towards those who were in rear parties or the RHQ and were never required to mount tanks to fight the enemy. Eyewitness accounts and the sudden disappearance of selected JCO/NCO on non-military tasks gave currency to these sordid tales. A fighting unit that had performed exceedingly well in combat was seized by this unfortunate crisis wherein the trust, command and control of officers on their troops and infighting among the officers broke the veneer of discipline and created a crisis of command. The junior officers stood disgruntled, watching this drama unfold. Months later, the new formation commander initiated court of inquiry proceedings. The subordinates, already splintered into groups, stood out as witnesses for the defence or prosecution, virtually breaking the backbone of the regiment. The more sensitive officers and the few with tarnished reputations found ways to delink from the regiment to find safer havens. Those who replaced them were the ones inducted from other regiments, or the clever cookies whose relations and friends had them posted away from combat zones. The end of the war saw the regimental reputation slide southwards. The actions of the mafia members made it abundantly clear that their association with 45 Cavalry was temporary and purely accidental. None had to serve longer with 45 Cavalry nor were they in for promotion or command. The unorthodox actions of some led to not only a crisis of command but finally to court martial.

Phoenix Syndrome

45 Cavalry was first raised on 3 August 1918 at Kantara, near Cairo (Egypt) and demobilized at Risalpur in 1919. It was re-raised at Meerut on 1 April 1941 and demobilized on 31 May 1946. The regiment was raised again as an Indian Cavalry Regiment on 16 May 1965 at the Delhi Cantonment. The re-raised history of the regiment never appealed to me, and I remember writing a brief poem titled 'Phoenix' in the regimental scrapbook. The title caught the imagination of all and continues to be used by the regiment till date as an informal descriptor. The phoenix is an immortal bird in Greek mythology which takes birth by rising again from the ashes of its predecessor. The events that were to unfold within the regiment in the coming months after the 1971 war once again brought it close to history repeating itself even while it had moved from the Eastern to the Western Front.

A regiment which had won laurels, recognition and gallantry

awards on the battlefield and reached the apogee of its performance in combat, had now succumbed to the greed of the mafia only to be dragged down to its perigee, even before reaching Suratgarh. The fabric of brotherhood and trust amongst officers had evaporated. While regiments like Poona Horse (17H) and Hodson Horse (4H) capitalized on their professional reputation and performance during the war, 45 Cavalry, despite having done as much and more, ruined itself due to the infighting. For nearly two years, it functioned like a headless chicken, facing inquiry for certain acts of omission and commission of certain officers. The summary of evidence progressed at snail pace followed by administrative action eating into their innards and destroying the fabric of regimentation.

Posted to 80 Armoured Delivery Regiment (ADR) located in Delhi in October 1971, I had volunteered to get back to the regiment before the start of the war. I believe it was an honourable decision in keeping with the military tradition of soldiering. I took leave in January 1972 to attend the wedding of a regimental officer in Delhi. During the pre-wedding cocktails, I overheard the officer's mother profusely thanking Major General Virendra Singh, the Colonel of the regiment, for having posted her son to 80 ADR in Delhi before the war (he was my replacement). General Virendra, acknowledged saying, 'Yes, you said he is your only son.' I was shocked, for I could never imagine that a regimental officer, six months my senior, had his mother arranging his posting and General Virendra acquiescing to such a request. A couple of weeks later, this officer was heard bragging at the bar that he had been graded with a 9-pointer (outstanding) by Digby in his Annual Confidential Report (ACR). This came as a rude shock to many frontline soldiers who, despite a sterling performance in battle, were labelled as 7/8-pointers in their ACRs. This was the first time in my life that I had witnessed how favouritism, duplicity and manoeuvring took place even at the regimental level. On reflection, I checked the posting in/out state in 45 Cavalry during the period preceding the declaration of war to find that two other officers had been posted out days before the regiment moved to the concentration areas. I was now beginning to understand that many decisions were indeed taken in the drawing rooms in Delhi and not in the war rooms of Army Headquarters. Despite all the years gone by, the truth in the above account holds good even today. My aim is not to denigrate or cast aspersions on any individual or unit, but to acquaint the readers with this reality of military existence.

Change of Command

Colonel R. N. Pandit, General Staff Officer, Grade 1(GSO-1) at ACC&S was posted to take over the command of 45 Cavalry. It appeared that such a posting suited his ambition and domestic bliss, as he was privy to the fact that this regiment was earmarked for relocation at Ahmednagar under the Southern Command. I was performing the duties of an adjutant when he arrived. He must have heard about my 'regimental reputation' from his circle of friends and others visiting ACC&S, for within a few days of arrival he asked me to hand over charge and lead a contingent for the farewell parade of the Army commander at Pune. No, this was not to be a mounted parade but an Armoured Corps marching contingent. The one thing that I hated the most while in the NDA was the drill square. The hate was to the extent that I was virtually the last in my batch to qualify for the drill square test. How the unit had been earmarked for this event even before being placed under the Southern Command was baffling. Notwithstanding my disinclination, I conducted regular drill practices at the Bombay Engineering Group Parade Ground at Kirkee. I led the regimental contingent at the farewell parade for General Sartaj Singh and was commended by the Parade

Commander Brigadier C. M. Campose and also by the Chief of Staff (COS) HQ Southern Command. Unknown to me, the COS wrote a demi official letter to the Commandant Brigadier Datar (CIH), expressing his appreciation at the standard of drill witnessed by the cavalry contingent.

The marching contigent was asked to proceed to Ahmednagar and take on the duties of the Advance party of 45 Cavalry. This is normal practice so that buildings and infrastructure allotted by the station headquarters to the unit is taken over before the arrival of the unit on permeant move. This was routine activity and completed satisfactorily. 45 Cavalry arrived at Ahmednagar, and within a few days, I was struck-off the strength of the regiment and detailed for the Advance Armoured Course at ACC&S. While still on the course, I was posted as Officer Commanding (OC) of the Range Wing at ACC&S. My total physical service under Colonel R. N. Pandit was less than a month. It was evident that he had used his influence to keep me out of the regiment during his tenure of command.

Wedding Bells

Brigadier I. S. Dhillon had taken over as the new commandant of ACC&S. The tankodrome project was complete. Lieutenant Colonel Guddi Grewal (later Lieutenant General), the senior-most bachelor in town, had just been promoted and moved to command an armoured brigade. Now, as the senior-most bachelor, I could claim the more spacious corner room in the cavalry mess. I devoted time to the *Cavalier* magazine, a journal of the ACC&S and also *Nagar News,* a monthly handout. One found enough time for golf and the library, and the evening used to be spent at the bar, followed by Chinese food at Annexe Café. On one such evening, a batchmate, Mobo Jadeja, turned up at the bar, accompanied by a tall, handsome figure. Jadeja introduced me to General Ghanshyam Singh, adding with great pride that he was his uncle. General Ghanshyam had been the erstwhile Commandant of ACC&S in 1956 and had introduced the famous Ghanshyam trophy, a silver Centurion Tank presented to an officer adjudged as the best young officer (YO) of the course. His name and reputation were a byword in the Armoured Corps. We had a couple of drinks together. I realized that he had a quiet dignity and manner that endeared him in the first meeting itself. After we had escorted the General to his room, Mobo told me how the General had looked after him and his mother (General Ghanshyam's sister) after she had been widowed. He spoke highly of General Ghanshyam's credentials—he was the son of Colonel Bapubha Gohil, Commander-in-chief of Bhavnagar State Forces, who, as OC of the Bhavnagar Lancers, had participated in the Battle of Haifa. General Ghanshyam was selected for training at Sandhurst in September 1927 and commissioned into the Black Watch Regiment in July 1929 as a King's Commissioned Indian Officer. Later, he joined 16 Light Cavalry in 1931 and was declared a Prisoner of War while serving in Burma. After commanding 2 Armoured Brigade and 43 Lorried Brigade, he was appointed Commandant of the Armoured Corps Centre and School. In 1955 when he received arrears for the period of incarceration in Changi Prison in Singapore as POW, he utilized it to set up the Ghanshyam Trophy. He later commanded 19 Infantry Division in Srinagar. Married to Immi, the daughter of Colonel Bakshi Chand, they had four children, two boys and two girls. While the boys schooled at Mayo College in Ajmer, the daughters finished school from Maharani Gayatri Devi Girls' School, Jaipur.

A few weeks later, Jayshree, his elder daughter, arrived at Ahmednagar to spend time with, Viloo Irani, a close friend of her parents . It was here that I met Jayshree and fell in love right away. She was tall, talented and beautiful—all solid reasons for me to give up my much-vaunted status as the senior-most bachelor and get married.

The wedding date was finalized for 7 March 1977. General Ghanshyam Singh and his family members had arrived at Ahmednagar. On 3 March 1977, a simple ceremony was to be conducted before the wedding. I woke up that morning with a slight pain in the stomach. I had promised to meet Major Ravi Bains and the regimental troops travelling by a military special tank train scheduled to leave for West Bengal early morning. The train's departure was delayed by over an hour. Despite the lingering pain, I kept strolling the platform with Ravi till the departure of the train. By now the pain had become intense. I returned home for a quick change and had to collect a package to be delivered to Mrs Ghanshyam Singh as the *tika* ceremony was scheduled for the same afternoon.

Mrs Ghanshyam, on seeing me, set the alarm bells ringing. 'Why do you look in pain?' I tried to brush it off, claiming that it was just a mild pain while simultaneously holding the left half of my stomach. 'No, it looks much worse, you must see a doctor.'

With that, a call went out to the Commandant Brigadier I. S. Dhillon. I was pushed into his staff car and driven off straight to the military hospital to be examined by the medical specialist. My elder brother, Shamsher, was there to listen in to the medical specialist's diagnosis. By the time the X-ray had dried, I was put on the seriously ill list due to an enlarged appendicitis in a critical state. Shammi signed the medical papers. By midday, I had been operated upon. Two days later, the specialist was back to help me take the first few steps post-operation. On 7 March, the marriage ceremony was conducted inside the medical ward! Keeping in view my medical condition and the fact that family members from both sides had arrived in station and invitations had also been sent out, it was mutually decided to make this a civil marriage. While the *pandit* and the guests had arrived, the Justice of the Peace (JP)[2] was playing truant. Brigadier I. S. Dhillon, bold as ever, had no hesitation in sending an armed guard to pick up the reluctant JP to register and certify the marriage. I was fit enough to take the traditional *pheras* around the fire but could not attend the evening function as I had still not recovered. Years later when I would meet those on the guest list, they would fondly share memories of the grand marriage attended by virtually every Armoured Corps family of Nagar, of the good wine, song, dance and music. Whenever I would claim, in all innocence, that I was not there, people would be shocked and sceptical as to how the bridegroom had not been present at his wedding. As I would tell them this story, they would wonder if I was pulling their leg, or was it that the whisky had erased their memory of having met the bridegroom, among the other four brothers present!

It was not long after the marriage that on completion of my Ahmednagar tenure, I was posted back to the regiment at Kanchrapara. It turned out to be the most depressing period of my life professionally. The same equipment, job, a dull routine, a one-street town and my wartime buddies mostly away made me miss the excitement of soldiering! What sustained me was my marriage and the birth of our two lovely children. I had reached the end of my professional soldiering. The boredom had set in, and the daily routine in a lifeless cantonment encouraged only drinking, gossip and basketball games with the troops. The long years doing regimental appointments, slow promotions, military routines in isolated cantonments, a strange level of chicanery and petty politics in the olive-green tribe was the proverbial last straw. My disgust was best reflected in my withdrawal from the Defence Services Staff College (DSSC) exam in the first year at Ahmednagar and then again next year when the permission to withdraw my name was withheld

[2] A court officer who can perform civil marriages

by the Commanding Officer. I had virtually signed off my military career by submitting blank answer sheets for the DSSC exams at Calcutta and later providing a written explanation for my conduct. I had lost the motivation for military service, having witnessed the conduct of regimental officers during and after the war. The court martials and the internecine private battles among officers and their conduct had made me wonder if at all I was serving in the Indian Army! The honour, fidelity and courage (*naam, namak, nishaan*) of the Indian Army, highlighted by Philip Mason in his book *A Matter of Honour* had evaporated. I was now beginning to look for an escape from the Army. It was then that I found out about the Cabinet Secretariat asking for volunteers in the rank of Major. I survived Kanchrapara to finally serve on deputation.

5

Deputation at RAW

I had completed 14 years of service in the Army. I had a good record of military service and a gallantry award, Mention in Despatches (MID), for my combat service during the 1971 war and a reputation as a good regimental officer. It was time to move to newer pastures, and RAW seemed like the perfect fit. The new job provided me with a desk, some dedicated staff and an office with a conducive work environment. My responsibility and duties relating to the branch were conveyed informally to me. As an experienced officer, one was expected to perform and uphold the good name and bring credit to the organization. One carried a key to his office; when one stepped out even briefly, he had to lock the door as part of the security regulations. The office timings were laid down and were adhered to; one had the freedom to function without anyone breathing down their neck. An atmosphere of self-discipline existed. There were no compulsory tea meetings, social calls, or any HR activity that would shackle or tie one down. I was also fortunate to have Brigadier Homji and Colonel Sawhney around, who neither imposed themselves nor made undue demands. The Naval Assistant Director Commodore

Radhakrishna and Air Force Assistant Director Wing Commander Sawant were both cerebral and helpful. There was no 'catch' in the work environment nor rank or authority dominating and polluting one's individuality or creativity. Though there were many negatives too, but I was prepared to overlook those instead of reverting to military service after my post-war military experience of attending the court martials of two commanding officers.

During induction, an 8-week intelligence course was conducted for a cross-section of officers from different services who had been inducted into the RAW. This was conducted at a separate safe house and included diverse subjects to make one fit for functioning undercover in embassies and high commissions abroad. The training ranged from face reading, memory, secret writing, shadowing, agent running to communication and other skills that form the bread and butter of sleuths. The most interesting time was spent on outdoor exercises and visits to special operation workshops where tools needed by agents and spies would be fabricated. The Army officers had to conduct few classes to acquaint the students with matters of military, organization, weapons and types of topographical information required for planning operations. Quite often, students would request instructors to narrate battlefield experiences.

We got to meet other officers posted at the Lodhi Road complex mostly during the weekly conferences of assistant directors (ADs) and above chaired by the Director of RAW. Each provided a gist of intelligence reports issued to the Service HQs, the Joint Intelligence Committee (JIC) or other important developments that needed the attention of all present. These meetings provided a learning opportunity and brought one up to date with both national and international developments. One always looked forward to briefings by stalwarts like B. Raman, K. N. Daruwala, Sanyal, as also the sharp incisive questions from others, especially Girish Chandra Saxena (Garry). I cannot recall a single occasion where anyone used his seniority or rank to silence others nor saw any efforts to publicly embarrass anybody. Even when a query could not be answered or an error was identified, it was handled in a civilized and sober manner but with the seriousness that it deserved. Good work was appreciated silently through the issue of a letter of appreciation to the officer by name or sometimes the branch. The weekly meeting brought many young talented ADs into closer contact. Some names that I can recall are Amber Sen, Rana Bannerjee, Amitab Mathur, Ajay, Ranade and Thukral. Major Mahajan and Dicky Verma were two officers who subsequently rose to occupy senior positions in the organization.

My deputation with RAW (Cabinet Secretariat) was to come to an end in 1984, since I had volunteered for a three-year tenure to serve as the Assistant Director. The Military Secretary Branch at the Army Headquarters had taken up a case for my reversion earlier than the completion of my tenure so that I could complete the Senior Command Course. This is a three-month compulsory course for selected majors who meet the criteria for command of units on promotion to the rank of lieutenant colonel. This entailed a reversion back to the Army from my current deputation. The then Director of RAW, N. F. Suntook, had vetoed this request by writing back to say that I had been assigned special duties of sensitive nature and could not be reverted. I was happy, as by now I was inclined to make a career with RAW, where a fresh cadre review was underway to screen volunteer officers on deputation from the central and state cadres. The officers on deputation were mostly from Indian Police Service (IPS), Indian Administrative Service (IAS), Indian Foreign Service (IFS), defence services and other Class A and B services of the Government of India.

The sensitive nature of my duties was linked to my manning the Bangladesh desk in RAW as also the appointment as Staff Officer to Director, RAW. Preparations for the 9th Asian Games, held in New Delhi from 19 November–4 December 1982 were in full swing. Some unconfirmed reports were beginning to circulate in the media that a segment of Sikhs would utilize this event to draw the world's attention to their cause of Khalistan—an embryonic movement with roots in the USA and Canada, demanding a separate homeland for the Sikhs in India. The RAW had an important role to play by providing inputs to the government. During one of the Asiad coordinating meeting, I had the opportunity of meeting Mr Arun Singh (later Minister of State for Defence), the Doon school buddy of Rajiv Gandhi. He held an important position in the organizing committee and was giving directions to other members involved in the planning and conduct of Asian Games. Since I was the Staff Officer to the Director of RAW, he was kind to make an offer of VIP passes for the games and invite me to partake of the lunch packets ordered from a five-star facility. He appeared like a powerful prima donna, who was friendly, informal and understood not only the mechanics of power but its discreet use and display.

I was not directly involved in any intelligence gathering action. The duty involved accompanying Mr Suntook for meetings within Delhi. This became a learning experience and an eye-opener on how the intelligence and counter-intelligence networks operated. I would sometimes be privy to radio calls relaying activities reported from targeted gurudwaras where any unusual activity or gathering of Khalistanis would come to notice. It never amounted to anything very exciting except the ride with the Director. This brief association made me aware of the poise and affable personality of Mr Suntook, who by dint of his ability and intelligence, was heading this premier organization, having been elevated from his parent service, the Indian Frontier Administrative Service.

After her return to power in 1980 as Prime Minister, Indira Gandhi brought back the first Director of RAW, R. N. Kao as the National Security Adviser. She had earlier formed the National Security Council in which many loyalists had been inducted. Garry

Saxena, an experienced and adroit IPS officer, had built a sterling reputation during the 1971 war and was brought in as the Additional Director. Grapevine suggested that he was earmarked to replace Mr Suntook as Director in due course. He had an affable and friendly personality, who was well respected in the organization. Unlike other police officers, he would mingle with juniors, meet socially and occasionally look forward to a game of golf. His poker face covered his penetrating questions and sharp intellect. He was well versed in all matters military, its organization and equipment.

The Bangladesh desk had separate military and political sections. Rana Banerjee from the IAS handled the political aspects. The reports coming in from various sources across the border, from our embassies and high commissions, or other agents deployed, would be handled at the desk level. Relevant information would be stored away in registers while current developments of significance disseminated through unofficial (UO) reports to the Service HQs and the Joint Intelligence Committee (JIC). The JIC would assess inputs received from other national agencies to prepare briefs for the National Security Adviser, Prime Minister's Office, among others. Relevant information would also be shared with the Ministry of External Affairs, paramilitary forces, directors of Army, Navy and Air Force intelligence, or other consumers on a 'need-to-know' basis. A summary of the UO issued would be shared during the weekly conference and intelligence gathered by RAW issued as a monthly digest. The 'need-to-know' principle would determine distribution. Close interaction existed between the political and military sections not only because the subjects were overlapping but more so because many ex-soldiers, freedom fighters and erstwhile members of the Mukti Bahini were political heavyweights who held sway over the Bangladesh government. Both Rana and I would interact in a friendly and cordial manner and when required put up important analysis to the Deputy Director or Joint Director.

The political and civil unrest in Bangladesh around mid-March in 1981 led to a regular stream of reports flooding the military and political desk at RAW. The sleeping cells, agents and informers had become hyperactive. The generally inert and easy-going embassy staff had come alive, sending detailed reports of developments taking place in Dhaka, military cantonments and within the political parties. The general talk within the office staff, consisting of experienced hands, was that most reports reaching the desk were not the result of any detailed investigation or based on documents or briefs received from moles in high places. Simply put, it was based on '*akhbaron se, ishteharon se, khyalon se*', meaning information culled from 'press reports, pamphlets and fertile imagination', which our overseas intelligence officers would submit as confidential reports received from reliable, undisclosed sources. The veracity could never be questioned, but the desk officer, with some experience, could separate the wheat from the chaff, and in 80 per cent of the cases, the 'precious' document went into the dustbin. Rarely would the reports contain inputs worthy of even being logged in the collation registers. As desk officers, when the ratio of unusable reports to collatable information based on the 80:20 principle changed, it indicated that developments of a more serious nature were taking place. The current trend of reports had swung towards the 80 per cent direction. The number of UOs initiated by the branch would go up and the members attending the weekly conference heard one with active interest—the senior among them perhaps seeking confirmation of the top-secret reports received by them from handlers of well-placed sources or moles.

Night of the Generals

Press reports of unrest and daily news and criticism of President Zia-ur-Rahman left no one in doubt that the outpouring was probably not another storm in the teacup. I was being flooded with reports from agents in the subcontinent regarding the ongoing activities of disgruntled colonels, majors and Mukti Jodhas (freedom fighters turned political leaders). Rana Banerjee and I were often burning the midnight oil to prepare intelligence reports and assessments of another coup in this already ravaged country. The Bangladesh coup on 30 May 1981 may have surprised citizens in India but certainly not the intelligence fraternity. An assessment of an imminent military coup in Bangladesh, jointly submitted by Rana and I, sent alarm bells ringing within the top echelons of RAW. The Deputy Director had read the report and questioned us at length before carrying the report directly to Director Garry Saxena. During the meeting with the Deputy Director, the background of some military commanders was discussed in an innocuous manner as also the discontented Bangladesh Nationalist Party (BNP) leaders, without giving away any concerns about the report submitted.

I was working late when I received a call from Mr R. Govindrajan[1], Additional Director, Special Services, asking me to meet the Director. I left for his office immediately. As I stepped in, Garry Saxena had just opened a small tin box to pull out a pinch of Pan Bahar, a type of mouth freshener. I had seen him do this sometimes during earlier meetings. Lying in front of Mr Saxena, on his large mahogany desk was an open file in a red folder. A lightweight aluminium toy, with a rider at either end, dipped to rise again, in slow motion in sync with the slow-moving fan, circulating the air. A miniature of the Big Ben stood at its usual place, next to multiple telephones. The clock alarm was always set to ring at an appointed time and served as a reminder to the visitor that the meeting was over. The Director signalled for me to take a seat while he brushed his hands to open

[1] Father of Dr Raghuram Rajan, former Governor, Reserve Bank of India

the folder. The light from the overhead lamp reflected off his large bald forehead as I waited for the alarm to ring. He raised his head, briefly to order a cup of tea for me. I was halfway through the cup of tea when he straightened up in his chair, his large frame now on display. He transfixed his eyes on me and in mild soft tones raised a few queries on some of the military personalities mentioned in the report. With a little twinkle in the eye and a smile, he got up to shake my hand. When I was halfway to the door he called out, 'Balram, let's play golf next Sunday.' This was the only occasion when the alarm did not announce the end of the meeting with the Director.

After taking over the Bangladesh desk as Assistant Director, I had studied old files, UO reports issued from 1971 onwards, dossiers along with the role of senior military officers serving in the Bangladesh Defence Forces. Separate files were maintained on important officers who were playing or likely to play an important role in their country. Information about the division commanders, brigade commanders, Mukti Jodhas and the change of command in units located in Dhaka were available in our collation registers. While studying the old reports of the assassination of Sheikh Mujibur Rahman, I came across information collated by RAW on the role of Zia-ur-Rahman. The dossier revealed important inputs on the planning and execution as well as the silent operators exercising the remote control on the execution being carried out. My interest focused on Zia-ur-Rahman as he was now the President and was also heading the BNP. It made for an interesting read.

Intelligence organizations the world over have never trumpeted their success stories because of the nature of work, while the media and the man on the street are ready to criticize failures, sometimes based on incomplete inputs. My own limited experience tells me that organizations like RAW are silent services and can rarely provide hard documented intelligence reports, but the consumer should be able to read 'between the lines' and comprehend the UOs initiated and be prepared to act on it without awaiting further corroboration, much like the general on the battlefield. The general with basic intelligence, study of the enemy tactics and organization, experience, intelligence inputs from troops in contact, neighbouring formations and higher headquarters will still never have corroborated intelligence about enemy deployment and reserves. There will always be gaps, and the desire for more corroborated information will never be fulfilled. The fluid nature of battle will never provide one the luxury of complete information. The decision must come from one's interpretation of the intelligence available and one's experience and reading of the battle. It is in such moments that one's leadership is put to test. An able general learns to synergize long years of study, experience and reflection to arrive at a decision which will lead to success.

Cadre Review—RAW

Some new developments at RAW had begun to change the way things were run here. Cadre review was now underway to fix the anomalies between the direct recruits in RAW, those from central services on deputation including the defence officers and the retired but re-employed. The major issue was the inter se fixation of seniority as also proportionate quota and terms of employment. The general feeling was that the IPS was calling the shots to the detriment of the rest. The direct recruits were amongst the more vocal ones. Two army officers also on deputation along with me had been carefully analysing the chances of our names being included in the cadre review that was now underway at RAW. One officer reverted to the Army as we wanted to take premature retirement. I was assigned the additional responsibility to look after the Pakistan desk. Around this time, the Army Headquarters sent fresh communication to RAW, demanding my reversion to the Army as my name had appeared in the list for the Senior Command Course the second time. The Director wrote back to say that they could not let me go as I held a sensitive appointment.

Besides the analysis of intelligence reports received from various agencies about important developments in Pakistan Army, the hot subject which was being handled by the senior officers was linked to the activities of Dr A. R. Khan, a nuclear scientist, and the progress made by Pakistan in assembling the 'Islamic Bomb'. While many of the secret reports never reached the Pakistan desk that I was handling, there was an understandable overlap as it related to Pakistan Army and the role of various general officers overseeing the project in Pakistan. The subject expert in RAW was Dr Santhanam, who would drop in to cross-check the background of certain officers or to verify locations of certain units linked with the development of the nuclear centre at Kahuta. Over a period of time, it led to watching videos or reading reports received by RAW on the activities of Dr A. R. Khan or the progress made by Pakistan—I would verbally share my comments with Dr Santhanam on each of these in the presence of a select team at the joint secretary level; there was no need to send written comments or assessments. My assessment was that Dr A. R. Khan had succeeded in his attempts, and sufficient indicators confirmed this belief that Pakistan was in possession of a low-grade nuclear device, indicators that Pakistanis were progressing rapidly to weaponize it before declaring the presence of Islamic bomb to take on the leadership of the Muslim world. That all this was part of holding a sensitive appointment did not cross my mind, as much of what we were discussing behind closed doors was also available to the international press and via multiple media reports.

By now, the overall working atmosphere within RAW had vitiated due to strikes by employees. Those at the forefront were direct entries voicing anger due to the disparity in pay, allowances, special pay, deputation allowance and the pensions that were being granted to the IPS cadre officers on deputation vis-à-vis the rest. The direct recruits, many of them handpicked from among friends and relations of those who had been inducted at inception in 1970, were a vocal and powerful lobby. As the RAW was essentially a police and intelligence bureau setup, the collective will of the IPS remained supreme. The sprinkling of IAS and IFS, or others on deputation, were mostly there out of their own choice or due to career options. The defence officers fell into three distinct categories—those who had joined during the first wave at the inception in 1970 were the best-off, enjoying the perks of defence and the largesse of the new service where good conduct led to foreign postings and promotions. The second category was those who had retired, and along with their pension, found an employment avenue with the option of a posting abroad by keeping their IPS bosses in good cheer. The last category comprised the fresh arrivals on deputation, who had to fill military intelligence desks at the Assistant Director level. This was the only government agency that viewed them as specialists, in a restricted sense. Those re-employed held sway over them, owing to their seniority and the fact that they had been in the business longer, providing them the opportunity to ride roughshod within the prevailing environment. The disgruntled amongst them would carry back tales of unfair practices and work environment at RAW and discourage fresh inductions. The Defence HQ would drag and delay the replacement of officers and finally release military deadwood, whose military career or service record was about to fold up, as part of perceived revenge. The inter-service relation between the Defence HQ and the RAW could change only when cordial relations developed between the top leadership.

The work on cadre review had progressed considerably. It appeared that a compromise formula had been worked out within which the concerns of the direct recruits had been considered and resolved. However, the stronghold of the IPS remained intact.

Service officers were provided with a choice where their military service would be slashed by a couple of years to ensure the pre-eminence of the IPS and direct recruits. This did not impact those who had joined the initial wave nor those employed on retirement. Having spent long years on peacetime duties with RAW, these early inductees were anything but army officers. They had turned into the civilians' politicians and sycophants. In such circumstances, few retained their military culture or character, as no one spoke about the harsh terms of loss in seniority offered to the army officers who were now applying for encadrement. Major General Taimani, who occupied the post of Chief Military Intelligence Officer, remained ambivalent. Our regular meetings with him produced no tangible outcome and his advice to revert to soldiering remained steadfast. He was subsequently appointed Special Defence Adviser to Malaysia.

My three-year deputation had spilled over into the fourth year in 1984. The two officers who were inducted along with me had since reverted to the Army. I was then holding dual charge for both the Pakistan and Bangladesh desks as no replacements had been provided by the Army to man these desks. The Military Secretary initiated a fresh signal asking for my reversion to join the Senior Command Course as failure would adversely affect my career prospects in the future. Director Garry Saxena had been appreciative of my work and had offered me a cadre post against the formula for relative seniority stipulated by RAW during our meeting. The application of this formula would have placed me relatively junior to many direct entries of IPS officers, even though I was now into my 17th year of commissioned service. My desire to continue with RAW was well known to Garry Saxena, and he, on his part, was supportive. But he cautioned me to say that the work of encadrement was still incomplete and would have to be approved by the government in due course. As Director, he would make a strong recommendation for my induction. However, he could not guarantee absorption as he would not remain Director forever. The reply to the Military Secretary was due in a few days. The choice before me was clear—resign from the Army to avoid reversion and hope to get absorbed into RAW, pending approval of the cadre recommendations by the government. Having explained the details, he made these notations on file and forwarded the case to Mr R. Govindrajan, Additional Director, Special Services. I left the Director's office satisfied, even a little happy, but also distressed at the way the dice had rolled for me.

Once home, I shared the news with my wife, Jayshree. Though she belonged to a military family, with a brother in 17 Poona Horse and her father, who retired as Major General from 16 Light Cavalry, she was neither excited about the offer nor the conditions under which we had spent nearly four years of our lives—living out of hostel accommodation in Pragati Vihar, near the Jawahar Lal Nehru Stadium. That said, the insecurity of leaving a permanent service to join RAW weighed heavy on her mind. The impact this decision would have on our school-going children would also be massive. My father-in-law had passed away a few months ago, and Jayshree's mother and brother were moving to Dharamshala. I spent the night tossing and turning, excited at the prospect of joining RAW, but financially insecure to face the risk. The next morning, I arrived at a decision (one that I have never regretted)—I must seek external counsel, and the first person I could think of was N. F. Suntook. After handing over charge of the Director, RAW, he now occupied an important post with the Government of India. I was able to get his contact details from the control room and called him. Fortunately for me, he picked up the call himself and immediately invited me over to his home near South Block. Mrs Suntook, an elegant lady, opened the door to welcome me into their home and offered me a cup of tea. After a few brief minutes, Mr Suntook arrived in his trademark Safari suit, cheerful as ever. Over a cuppa, I explained all that I was told by Garry Saxena. He heard me out and finally asked a few questions:

'How many years have you served in the Army?'

'Have you cleared your compulsory examinations?'

'Will you pick up your next rank in the Army?'

'How many years is it before you complete pensionable service?'

His questions helped me gain the clarity that I needed. He made it abundantly clear that till I had completed a minimum of 20 years of pensionable service, there should be no question of switching horses midstream. This was doubly important as the children were still very young. Secondly, the Army had clearly stated that the failure to attend the Senior Command Course, after the third nomination, could go against my future prospects. The cadre review was an exercise in progress, the finalization and final approval of which, he felt, would probably still necessitate amendments once the government approved of it. On hearing that my prospects for further promotion were still favourable, he advised with certainty and said, 'In that case, you must revert.' Finally, he added that he was aware of my profile, and my service record with RAW and that as an organization, it would expand in the coming years. It would need good officers in the future too, and with my record and experience, I stood a better chance to come back.

'Take my advice, and do not resign from the Army. Get back. Finish your course and pick your promotion in the Army.'

I heaved a sigh of relief. I thanked them for their warmth, hospitality and the valuable guidance. I returned home to share the mature advise received and the assurance that I could revert to RAW after completing my pensionable service. I was confident that it would bring some cheer to my wife. I spent a sleepless night, tossing and turning the advice tendered. The thought that I was favourably placed to take the plunge now by risking a career with RAW against the security of pension and family responsibilities led to the feeling of 'so near and yet so far', which still bugged me like a virus, though good sense cautioned me from following that path.

I still had a few days before communicating my decision on the offer made by Garry Saxena. I was convinced that the advice tendered by Mr Suntook was the best for me. The only bit bugging me was returning to the olive-green uniform. Over the last few years, I had worked hard to create an alternative. Could there be an alternative still? Frantic, I decided to call on the Colonel of the regiment of 45 Cavalry. In 1971 a similar initiative had helped me in re-joining the regiment within three days of my posting to New Delhi. Like a drowning man clutching on to a straw, next morning without further thought, I proceeded to the office of the Military Assistant to the COAS. I met General A. S. Vaidya in his office and brought to his notice the offer of my induction into RAW made by Garry Saxena. The option of permanent secondment to another service was not uncommon and was within the powers of the COAS as the Ministry of Defence (MoD) policy permitted serving officers to be seconded to the Defence Research and Development Organisation (DRDO) and a few other government offices. He heard me patiently and then mentioned that the Military Secretary (MS) had taken a decision not to permit the secondment of Army officers to RAW. I then requested for extension of my deputation, till the completion of 20 years of pensionable service, as a last-ditch effort, which, too, was turned down. He mentioned that a request for extension of deputation had been received from RAW, but the Military Secretary had recommended a rejection and obtained the approval of the previous COAS. I had reached the end of the line as no further possibility existed. With grim reality staring me in the face, I was in the act of taking leave when the Chief gestured that I remain seated. A faint glimmer of hope appeared. While I sipped tea and answered his questions on the nature of work done with RAW, he suggested that as a good regimental officer I should recommend another regimental officer to the post that I would vacate. The only name of a regimental officer and a possible contender that I could recall was his son-in-law. I blurted out, 'Oh, you mean help Cocky?' 'No, his name is Arun, not Cocky,' came the quick retort. I swallowed the snub, and quickly corrected myself, 'Yes, of course, Arun Kochhar.' The reality hit me like a tonne of bricks. I had taken a plunge to sort out my secondment to the RAW and here I was in a bargain with the Colonel of my regiment to help his son-in-law replace me in the same post! Was this a nightmare? How could I have helped him? The dilemma could only be answered in the affirmative as by now I began to gasp for breath. I agreed to do my best and left, thanking him for the cup of tea he had so generously offered.

Two days later I met Garry Saxena in his office to share with him my meeting with Mr Suntook and my acceptance of his advice not to resign but to revert. He confirmed that Mr Suntook had spoken to him too and had been given the assurance that I could revert to the RAW at a later date. He mentioned that the Army had turned down all requests for secondment and was also reluctant to send officers on deputation. I then brought up the subject of Major Arun Kochhar as a likely replacement for my post. With great glee, I told him that the candidate I was sponsoring was the son-in-law of the current COAS. This brought a glint of admiration to Garry Saxena's eyes as if I had conducted a well-planned intelligence operation by talent-spotting a valuable target. He had a few questions that I answered about General Vaidya and his family. He got up to shake my hand, thanked me and quickly added, 'But please tell the general we will make the officer sit through a written test.' In time, Arun Kochhar wrote the in-house written examination, was interviewed by the Additional Director and despite my detailed briefing, failed to qualify and was therefore rejected. Years later, when Garry Saxena was appointed as the Governor of Jammu and Kashmir, I met briefly in Delhi. We spoke about the success of 1981, Operation Vanishing Cream and the golf games we had played together. He was happy to learn that I had been promoted as Brigadier.

I had the opportunity of interacting with all three Service HQs, Ministry of External Affairs, Border Security Force and Joint Intelligence Committee. I had met and interacted with joint directors and the Director several times within the organization. As the organization functioned on a 'need to know' basis, the chain of command and reporting channels were flexible. On many occasions, my immediate superior would be unaware of special tasks that were being allotted to me, yet they would not spike one for information. Such work was dutifully recognized, and often, a brief congratulatory letter of appreciation would appear by name or addressed to the branch. Special comments on letters received from the MEA or the Service HQs would bring cheer to the staff who had worked, in army parlance, 'beyond the call of duty' to make that report or document valuable. On special occasions a report submitted on file would need to be discussed with the Director and a summary or a one-page draft report submitted by hand 'for your eyes only' would be carried by the Director to the PMO or a visiting dignitary.

The deputation phase added to my experience. I was able to understand and appreciate the world outside the Army. Working in a mixed group of talented personnel inducted from IPS, IAS, IFS, scientists, direct cadres, research officers and many lesser-known streams was excellent. This pool of talent had some of the most outstanding IPS officers whose sense of commitment and patriotism was the best that I had been exposed to. Most of the officers that I came across were sincere and hardworking. Overall, one found oneself in a very conducive and happy working environment where too much regulation and rank syndrome did not exist. One was free to voice one's opinion and could wield one's pen to make one's point without the fear that the next superior would cast it into the bin. Rewards and recognition were not denied to those on deputation. However, who was related to whom, and whose relatives and friends were sitting in which ministry made a capital difference in one's work and postings. The younger set of IPS officers and direct entries would spend time planning their next posting. The MEA was their constant bitch. Comparison with the perks enjoyed by Defence Forces was another pet hate. There was, however, appreciation for the work and efficiency of the Defence Forces. Many would take pride in narrating their stint with the NCC while in school or college as well as the compulsory attachment to units, and quite often incidents of co-op and help received when deployed in the forward areas and border districts as well. They displayed a high sense of self-discipline. It was the only office where the service officer was viewed as a specialist in his field and treated accordingly. Many of them had served in different capitals of the world. Their general knowledge, awareness, car models, gadgets, travel and holiday plans, postings, scandals and recent acquisitions were the small talk instead of the mountain peak climbed, the field area visited, their regimental life and inspections. Inter-service rivalry and rank parity were hotly contested. At a personal level, one found oneself more confident and capable and could win respect and adoration for small tasks, which, to us, appeared routine in the regimental life.

I had worked hard while on deputation and had received recognition and appreciation for the work I had done. More than that, I now carried the rich experience of working in a multi-disciplinary organization that was not only the eyes and ears of the government but also its brains, influencing policy and strategic thought. The assurance that I could revert at a future date—a word of honour of two outstanding directors of the RAW—was a spinoff benefit That I was personally satisfied and felt more confident and better equipped to revert to soldiering were valuable accomplishments from my deputation.

6

Raising the Regiment

Senior Command Course

After a few days in the regiment, I proceeded to Mhow to attend the Senior Command Course. A batch of about 60 officers, many of whom were course mates or officers I had known or met either in the NDA, IMA, during military exercises, or the war, were present. This made the transition from RAW back to the Army easier and more enjoyable. The course was packed with officers who had Previous Course Knowledge (PCK) to help them sound more professional and cerebrally better equipped to perform the roles of unit commanders and military leaders. I found this an abhorrent and demeaning practice that helped one to tide over vague and mundane military teachings. I concentrated on staying fit as per military standards and spent more time reading whatever caught my fancy in the library. Most of the military sand model discussions on different operations of war were repetitions of what had been played out two or three courses earlier, with a few modifications. The PCK category, many of them carrying the much-hyped 'passed staff college' (psc) qualification, would take centre stage and score brownie points. I sat patiently through these periods, speaking only when I had some valid point to contribute or respond to a question that was asked. During heated debates engineered by the experienced directing faculty, one would finally arrive at answers and deductions given out in printed sheets to the directing faculty. My experience of war and reading of military history had taught me that in the Army what the general proposes, fate disposes. When on the battlefield, there were only four choices: one stops where one is, one beats a retreat, one breaks through the centre or one turns the flank. The rest was all poppycock! In war, the plan does not matter so much as its execution. The armoured officers fared well due to the work culture and ethos emulated during their regimental service, which gave full scope to subalterns to retain their individuality. It also encouraged young officers to read biographies and personal experiences of the great commanders of war. In the study of military leaders and military history, the focus should be on the reactions of the commanders to the crisis and how they overcame it, instead of details of incidents that were less important. Such study shaped the mental attitudes to develop flexibility and self-reliance and build a buoyant and well-rounded personality. Presence of mind is a vital attribute of a leader. It comes through preparation and knowledge of the environment in which one is deployed and a general awareness of the terrain, technology, enemy and location. Young minds get conditioned by this as they grow in service. A good knowledgeable cavalry officer does not have to consciously think of a solution; it is already on his fingertips. This was evident during the Senior Command Course where most kept a mature and balanced profile.

A few weeks into the course, a major development had erupted in the country. The Akali Dal President H. S. Longewal had invited the militant religious leader Jarnail Singh Bhindranwale to take refuge inside Amritsar's Golden Temple Complex to avoid arrest. Bhindranwale had converted this into an armoury and his headquarters. As a result, the military had to be called in and Operation Blue Star was carried out from 1–8 June 1984 to remove Bhindranwale and his followers from the buildings of the Harmandir Sahib Complex within the Golden Temple. The electronic media and the press covered these developments widely. Sikh troops and their families were understandably influenced by all that the media was reporting. The ingredients that make a mutiny probable were rapidly developing in the units with Sikh troops. The simmering discontent of what was happening in towns and villages severely impacted the soldiers too, as no one can remain impervious to these developments. Many would sympathize and express themselves. In units where officers were alert and had a good understanding and a two-way communication channel, the facts of the matter could be explained better along with the actions undertaken by the government. In some units, this simmering discontent was overlooked, and the officers failed to assuage or guide the sense of hurt that the troops had been experiencing, thereby permitting the anger and discontent to explode into killings and mayhem.

Operation Blue Star was launched by the Western Command to evict the militants out of the sacred compound. The military action was criticized by Sikh officers, and many soldiers from Sikh units deserted them. The KGB (Komitet Gosudarstvennoy Bezopasnosti) of Russia had warned India that the CIA (Central Intelligence Agency) and ISI (Inter-Services Intelligence) were working together and had recruited over a thousand Special Services Group commandoes to spread across the countryside and destabilize the government. The warnings did not lead to preventive action or resolution. Finally, tanks and guns were utilized to flush out the militants at a heavy cost to life, limb and property. Some semblance of order and normalcy would return in due course. The Sikh sentiments were badly hurt, and some of the officers attending the course vented their feelings by seeking interviews with the commandant with requests to 'return to unit'. The course was not curtailed but Operation Blue Star impacted the class composition of new raisings, as I was to learn soon.

Thoughts Before the Raising

I had been entrusted the task of raising a new regiment—13 AR. However, as I awaited firm orders, I found myself with a few weeks to reflect and plan how I would go about it all. During this period, I was attached to the Basic Training Regiment, commanded by Colonel Narjinder Singh of Skinner's Horse. The three most important thoughts on my mind were the superstition associated with number 13, handling of the new class composition and the discredited equipment—the Vijayanta tank allotted to the regiment. The negative opinion on the Vijayanta was unanimous within the Armoured Corps—a good gun but an unreliable engine, operationally third rate, lack of engine power, untrustworthy transmission and clogged filters being its major problems. This unwieldy 40-ton monster, fitted with a 105 mm gun and Leyland L60 diesel engine fared poorly compared to the Russian tanks in use. It was built at Avadi, Chennai, India, based on a licensed design of Vickers Mk 1 of UK. Under project Bison, some modifications had been undertaken, but the confidence level and opinion of tank crews, especially the drivers remained unchanged. This would be a critical area as lack of confidence in equipment would affect battle efficiency and morale. This was India's first indigenous tank and had been in service for a couple of years.

My parent regiment had a class composition of two-third South Indian Classes (SIC) and the remaining one-third was Other Indian Classes (OIC), a euphemism for all those not categorized as martial classes by the British. This was the only OIC squadron raised post-independence in 1965. My experience, management skills and leading SIC/OIC in 45 Cavalry would be at variance while handling the Sikhs and Rajputs. The customs and traditions of each class and community are fundamental to personnel management and require sensitive handling. During the 1971 war, a troop of Sikhs and Rajputs of 63 Cavalry had served under me, briefly, during the Tank versus Tank Battle at Garibpur. This did not amount to much, but it served as a reference point during personal interactions. The bigger and far more relevant issue was the aftermath and the impact of Operation Blue Star on the troops. The realization that no new armoured regiment had been raised since 1971 was significant. Each regiment would have accumulated a set of 'bad hats' and 'disciplinary cases' during the preceding 13 years, who were available to be syphoned off to new raisings. Of special concern was the Sikh component, whose role during the fall out of Operation Blue Star would remain undocumented. The manpower for new raisings is provided by milking existing JCOs, NCOs and crew members of all trades from existing regiments. That regiments could offload the less desirable members falling within the criteria for posting to new regiment laid down by the record office and instructions of the Director General Mechanised Forces was unavoidable. I visited the Chief Record Officer (CRO) to understand the criteria laid down for the posting of All Ranks to a new raising. On the point of principle, I decided not to interfere or request any change or influence decisions.

Having been commissioned into a new raising in 1966, I was privy to commanding officers and empanelled officers approaching the MS branch to remove or add names of officers to draft panels earmarked for posting to a new regiment. Each armoured regiment has a colonel of the regiment and a senior officer to guide and oversee the interest of his regiment. Sometimes, officers and the JCO would use this route to get a favourable decision for reversion.

Knowing what havoc such canvassing can create, I abstained from this practice and kept clear of the MS branch. I chose not to tinker with the panel of officers or men posted despite local advice to the contrary. This decision revealed an unusual insight, one that I had acquired rather unintentionally from the SIC personnel of 45 Cavalry. Numerous SIC personnel had voluntarily opted for a posting to 13 Armoured Regiment. This was brought to my notice by one JCO from my earlier regiment. This piece of information served as a balm for my bruised ego. However, my mind hesitated to digest this. A deeper analysis revealed that promotions in units having SIC component had become stagnant in older regiments, especially in 45 Cavalry during the preceding years, due to changes in manpower policies of recruitment and a ban on new raisings. That a few may have actually volunteered to join 13 Armoured Regiment due to their affection for me remained a distinct possibility. However, the larger motivation of quicker promotions was a reality. That I had not used influence to induct a few handpick favourites helped my reputation for fair play.

I availed my free time in the ACC&S library to research the class composition of 13 Armoured Regiment. I also compared the class composition of the existing regiments to that of 13 Armoured Regiment, only to find that not a single regiment was organized with a similar class composition having Sikhs, Rajputs and SIC in the same regiment. This held true for regiments raised post-independence as well. I went through manuals and books on the Indian Army, many written by the British, to understand if such a composition existed during the world wars or even during an earlier period of history. It transpired that there was no documented evidence or reference to a combination of Sikhs, Rajputs and SIC being grouped under one regiment. The CRO had searched old records but drew a blank. I was determined to utilize this uniqueness once the raising commenced.

The myth of number 13 intrigued me. I was aware of the common belief that it was unlucky, because at the time of Jesus Christ's Last Supper, there were 13 people around the table, counting Christ and the 12 apostles, but the one to betray Jesus was Judas Iscariot, the 13th to sit at the table. Literature also supports this view, as witnessed in the Shakespearean play *Julius Caesar*, where 13 conspirators, led by Brutus, carry out the execution of Julius Caesar. However, Hindus believe the 13th day of every month is dedicated to Lord Shiva, and therefore consider it to be extremely auspicious. The number 13 also holds special significance for Sikhs, with the harvesting festival of Baisakhi celebrated every year on April 13 as also the creation of Khalsa or Pure Sikh. The eagle in the American seal carries 13 olives and 13 arrows in either hand. However, the number 13 has been avoided as a practice in the Air Force and Navy and rarely been accepted by Army units. In civil establishments too, the number 13 is generally avoided. Thus, it was quite likely that the personnel reporting for duty would carry this baggage of doubt and superstition along with them. Quite obviously, the number 13 became a subject of great interest to me.

The 'fixed class' composition introduced by the British following the War of Independence in 1857 was discarded, and all new units raised between 1971 and 1983 were to have manpower on an 'All India, All Class' principle as the approved policy of the government. This meant that new units would have a mixed class composition. However, since Operation Blue Star had a massive impact on Sikh sensibilities, it had led Sikh troops in some units and subunits to revolt. Thus, General Vaidya, the Chief of Army Staff, had advocated that new units be raised with a homogeneous class composition at the subunit level, which found favour with the government. As a result, the government rescinded the earlier order of 'All India, All Class' and reverted to raising new units on the revised pattern of a 'fixed class' at the subunit level. Thus, 13 Armoured Regiment became the first armoured regiment to be raised after 13 years with a unique class composition of SIC, Sikhs and Rajputs. The realization that I was being asked to raise an armoured regiment in the aftermath of the 1984 Operation Blue Star, during which Sikh uprisings had been reported by the national media, added to the responsibility that was thrust upon me. It was fair to assume that this new raising would have to brace itself against 'disoriented' manpower as regiments would utilize this opportunity to clean their Aegean stables. As the Sikh psyche was visibly disturbed, I realized that some measures would have to be taken to assuage the sense of hurt amongst the Sikh personnel. Confidence building and balance within the three classes were essential to make the unit a composite and effective team.

As far as the equipment was concerned, the only inference I could reach was that despite all its drawbacks and the maligned reputation of the Vijayanta, it was an indigenous tank. That we could manufacture a tank despite being a Third World country was in itself a matter of pride. The drawbacks were being addressed and a special project to upgrade the engine had been functional for some time. The challenge I was faced with was to ascertain ways to convince the officers and tank crews not to accept the prevailing Nagar view, as it would prove disastrous for the regiment under raising. As I could do nothing to alter the physical or technical parameters of the Vijayanta, I decided to change the perception of the regiment by referring to the Vijayanta as the best-known tank of the Third World, which had the most accurate 105 mm gun. There was truth in this statement, as the world viewed India to be part of the Third World, struggling with its economy and poverty. Further, the gestation period of making a tank from the drawing board to the final induction could take two to three decades even in advanced countries. As a result, our defence scientists and the DRDO had done a fair job against this backdrop. The shortcomings would be overcome as many projects for upgrading the Vijayanta were in progress. As users, we could take pride in the belief that the Vijayanta was the best that the Third World had produced. To translate this thought and convince the tank crews, especially the drivers, we needed attention and maintenance of a high order.

On 10 December 1984, I was to attend a meeting chaired by the Director Armoured Corps Major General J. M. Vohra at New Delhi regarding raising of the regiment. Major General Hanut Singh, MVC, Deputy Director Military Operations (DDMO[B]) along with representatives of Weapons & Equipment-14 (WE-14), EME (ops) and SD4 and the Commandant of 8 Cavalry were also present. The policy letter on raising listed out details of the issue of vehicle and store, indenting for stores from different depots, the release of a training grant, move of 15 Vijayanta tanks of 8 Cavalry and the assistance for conversion training. The government letter, along with the minutes of the meeting, were issued soon after to all addresses to facilitate and release the indented items. The meeting also provided an opportunity to meet the Director Armoured Corps (DAC) and officers posted under him, who in the coming months would interact and facilitate the growth of the regiment by coordinating progress. Major General Hanut spent a few brief minutes talking about Major Narag, my erstwhile squadron commander during the Tank versus Tank Battle of 1971, in which he was martyred. He recalled Narag's prowess in football as a young officer of Deccan Horse and narrated an incident when, as his gunnery instructor, he had pulled up Narag for a minor breach committed during a training session in his class.

The Delhi conference acted as a confidence-building measure and helped me share my concerns and project my point of view. After all, personal meetings were always helpful in achieving cooperation and reducing friction when a large project is underway. I returned from Delhi, renewed and ready to take the task of raising a regiment head on. It was a welcome challenge that would test my creative spark. While the headquarters had planned and coordinated details for raising the regiment, I would have to ensure that there were no gaps in on-ground execution to determine the final outcome. The realization that the new raising had less money, resources and cohesion implied greater reliance on the creativity of the manpower. My experience as a subaltern in 45 Cavalry had taught me that when one had less, individuals became more inventive and had more fun because one valued what one had. With these thoughts in mind, I put pen to paper to draft my first letter to all officers on the panel of 13 Armoured Regiment, so that each one received the demi-official letter well before they were struck off strength of the current unit. The following letter was posted to each officer on the panel of 13 Armoured Regiment.

Lieutenant Colonel B. S. Mehta
13 Armoured Regiment
Commandant
c/o AC Centre & School
Ahmednagar
1301/A

13 Armoured Regiment will come into existence at 1100 hours on 21 December 1984 after invoking the blessings of the Almighty. It joins the proud ranks of Armoured Corps units whose rich heritage, custom and tradition will form the backbone of our growth and commitment to excellence. Our immediate task will be to complete the raising within the specified period and become battle worthy. This is a challenging and interesting task. It demands of us unstinted loyalty, hard work and soldierly dedication to make this regiment a hard-hitting and efficient fighting machine. For this endeavour, the country and the Army will be providing us with the sophisticated, indigenously produced best-known tank of the Third World—Vijayanta! It also provides a balanced, distinguished and loyal class composition consisting of Sikh, Rajput and SIC. This is a unique combination, being the first of its kind not only within the Corps but throughout the history of our Army. The man and machine being both par excellence, it will be our bounden duty as commissioned officers to put our heads and expertise together to mould this into a regiment of repute so that it becomes the toast of this elite Corps and a symbol of death and disaster for the known and emerging enemies of our great country.

You are coming to the 13th from a very fine and renowned regiment. Like all good soldiers, you did not volunteer for this change. Change for us has been determined by a superior authority—perhaps for a good reason. As change is not due to own volition, it takes the form of being preordained. The other name for this is destiny—call it kismet. While we choose friends based on mutual affinity, destiny determines our brother. This is what we will be to each other in the coming days. This relationship is strong and binding and sustains itself for a life span. It grows stronger with each passing day. Brotherhood will become the reality of our new existence. The goodness and happy memories of your present regiments are assets of this new brotherhood which you will bring along. You must share these assets with the rest and thereby strengthen yourself to make us stronger and tensile. As a founding member you are an important pillar on which the edifice of the 13th will be raised. This will call for sacrifices, cooperation and mutual interdependence—in short, the total of goodness acquired in the parent regiment. So, bring these assets and remember to share your joys, hopes and fears and thereby create a spirit of mutual respect and accommodation from the day of your arrival. If we can do this, I assure you we will not only complete the assigned task within the shortest possible time but have a jolly good time doing it.

Lastly, most of you are not unaccustomed to the regimental life and are generally conversant with duties you must be already performing. Organizational changes, being few between your old and new regiment, there is every likelihood of you being assigned similar duties. You could help us by coming fully armed with the wherewithal (tools of your trade) be it standing orders for peace and war, SOPs, GS publication, manuals, documents, vehicle modification details, precis, training aids, etc. Do bring along donations your regiments have agreed to make, buttressed through friendly persuasion if possible. A new regiment needs everything from a pin to a tank. Bringing along the first may be hazardous (pins prick) whereas the second may embarrass the present CO into signing a loss statement. You have my permission to bring everything useful that exists between these two limits.

I wish you and your families a Merry Christmas and a Happy New Year. For those of you who wish to bring your families, permission is granted and accommodation assured. Inform us of your ETA and specific requirements, if any.

The coming year and the 13th will bring you good luck and plenty of cheer.

Till we meet,

Best wishes,

Balram

Major General K. M. Dhody, Commandant ACC&S, was under posting, soon to be replaced by Major General G. S. Kler (later Lieutenant General). Prior to departure, he held a mini conference, wherein his staff officers briefed me of the administrative arrangements made to assist the regiment. This included the essentials of immediate support required in terms of clerical staff, furniture, vehicle and accommodation. He congratulated me on my appointment and handed over a cheque of ₹2,000 as the compulsory contribution of the centre for new raisings. As the Colonel of 73 Armoured Regiment, he offered a shortlist of Sikh risaldar majors from his regiment for my consideration. My request for repair of the tent replacement hut (TRH) accommodation was accepted. The next day, an officer and the maintenance engineer from the GE office accompanied me for inspection. The TRH was a bare shell constructed with prefabricated cement blocks and asbestos sheets for roofing and bare essentials of fitment, furniture and plumbing. Notwithstanding the quality of construction, it was considered a boon by those who had grown up living in tents and makeshift bathrooms. TRH was a priority for me as many officers and personnel would be reporting for duty from field areas and non-family stations. The raising was to be completed within six months so that a well-maintained TRH accommodation could be allotted on arrival to all those desirous of bringing their families.

Nucleus Arrives

By the third week of December 1984, the nucleus staff had started arriving. A reception party, with transport, had been placed at the railway station to welcome the new arrivals. The majority had made their own arrangements through regimental affiliations. A small makeshift office had been set up within the TRH complex, and a landline telephone was installed. I had vacated my single officers' accommodation and moved into the TRH. Replies to my demi-official letter sent earlier had also been received. Reading the list of empanelled officers, I realized that I would be meeting most for the first time. The next few weeks would be the test of my ability to comprehend non-verbal communication during meetings. Like a horse senses the energy of its rider or a dog the movement of its owner, the soldier must learn to read these signs. Someone who is ingratiatingly effusive with flattery may be hiding hostility and ill will. While you do not have to mistrust all friendly gestures, one needs to be wary of unusual chumminess and excessive praise. I decided to write my first impressions of each officer and re-read them after a gap of 6–8 weeks to judge my own ability.

I vividly remember my first meeting with most officers and the first few words exchanged. No one likes to be cast off by his parent regiment. While some carried the baggage of disappointment, others tried to display maturity by not mouthing the hurt of having become superfluous to the previous regiment. Some harboured the hope of early reversion based on assurances provided by 'military connections'! Nobody expressed happiness at his transition to 13 AR, but still accepted it due to obedience and a sense of military duty. A few figures, however, stood out more prominently. One was Major Randhir Singh, posted as the regiment's second-in-command (2IC). Within minutes of our first meeting, he told me he had no ambitions of promotion, or the desire to command the regiment in the future. He had burnt his boats for his next rank due to bad ACRs. 'Leave me out of professional duties, I will cover all administrative tasks,' he said. I appreciated his frankness as well as his implicit faith. He appeared proud of his Rajput heritage and his Mayo School background. He was a little slovenly in his dress and deportment but clear-minded and forthright in expressing his opinions. The squadron commanders Major Virendra Singh, Major Mir Ahmed Shah and Major Vinod Kochhar appeared more circumspect and cautious. The first interaction with them was more formal. Their hesitation to open up would take longer due to the age and seniority differential. It was, however, evident that Virendra was, by nature, an introvert while Vinod was more effusive and forthcoming. Mir could be easily identified as an extrovert and a sportsperson. Major Saurabh Butalia, who joined later, was a lanky Sikh who had spent long years stationed in Ambala. He was affable and courteous but guarded in his views that he expressed in a languorous drawl. Overall, I was satisfied that the regiment had been blessed with above average, hardcore and talented officers, who, while retaining their individual characteristics, had begun to blend into a fine team and served as pillars on which the edifice would grow.

Among the rest of the team, one name that comes forth is Major S. D. Sayal, who was posted as quartermaster (QM). There was no formal meeting with him. On day one of his arrival, he had borrowed some wooden crates and a folding stool for a table and chair to set up a small working office and was in dialogue with the clerk attached from the Station HQ, when I spotted a new face in the office TRH block. He jumped out of his seat to introduce himself. He was a special list commissioned officer, who had risen from the ranks and had served as quartermaster in two units. He was about ten years older than me and was as fit as a fiddle with a cheerful demeanour. Amongst the younger lot were Mantaj, Manbir, Ravi Dhillon, K. K. Chowdhary, Shah, Keju Yadav, Shashank Yadav, Ajay Arora, Sengupta, Pradeep Samyal, S. N. Jha and Ajay Gupta. Besides meeting each one personally, I read through their record files and biodatas to ascertain the allotment of squadrons and appointments depending on the individual officers' professional qualifications. Randhir's advice and recommendation was valuable during this exercise, as he had personnel knowledge in a few cases.

The first batch of approximately 80 JCOs/ORs (Other Ranks) had arrived in small groups. The key regimental appointments were assigned to develop a regimental skeleton and Squadron Headquarters for the semblance of a functional unit. Allotment of personnel to squadrons was unnecessary, since it was a homogenous class composition at the squadron level, except transferring a few to the composite HQ squadron while the others adopted the standard designation of 'A', 'B' and 'C' Squadrons. Initial work centred around the preparation of standard operating procedures (SOPs) for regimental institutes, office procedures, preparation of indents for the demand of stores, vehicles, equipment authorized on the War Establishment Tables from different depots and ordnance factories, correspondence with different units and headquarters for the release of manpower and other multifarious funds such as annual training grant, annual contingency grant, including ₹500 per armoured regiment based on the standard contribution approved by the DAC.

After the arrival of the nucleus staff, a welcome regimental get-together was organized for all the ranks. The officers moved around to meet and greet each other as also the newly posted personnel. Looking at their dress, turnout, qualification and operational experience made me appreciate the selection criteria laid down by DAC (now the Directorate General of Mechanised Forces) and the Armoured Corps records. At the first meeting with this cross-section of SIC, Sikhs and Rajputs, I realized that much like the officers, the JCOs and NCOs were unhappy being transferred out from their previous units. These simple individuals had retained their sense of pride and followed orders. It was now my responsibility to create a happy work environment to improve their outlook, overcome the initial disappointment and utilize their talent and potential for the good of the unit.

As a subaltern in 45 Cavalry, I had been privy to officers and JCOs applying for reversion to parent units. Though the current lot of troops felt dejected, none expressed distress or a request to revert to the parent regiment. This was a major change to my recall of 45 Cavalry. To me, they collectively represented a pool of professional talent. As is not unusual, many talented JCOs/NCOs, with the natural potential for leadership, had been victimized and posted out by units in the attempt to clear their own stables. My service and experience had taught me that many discards were unpolished gems. One of the primary tasks of command, in fact the secret to being a good commander, is talent spotting. Once identified, these 'movers and shakers' would become my talent pool, if properly harnessed. One active, motivated and energetic right-thinking JCO/NCO can infuse an excellent spirit into his comrades and become a positive influence on the troop or the appointment assigned to him.

Those gathered for tea could be divided into three distinct groups based on the equipment held by their previous regiments—T54/T55 regiments, Vijayanta regiment and those who had served in both. Those from units holding the Russian T54/T55 were open in their criticism of the Vijayanta, deeming it undependable. This was further confirmed by those who had experienced the truth of this tank's reliability. Everyone felt apprehensive about the Vijayanta tank. The only ones who still had a good word were from the gunnery trade, who felt that it outmatched the performance of the earlier Centurion tank. The concern was palpable as tank crews spend long hours on training and maintenance and know the equipment better than they know their wives. Battlefield survival is linked with superior technology and training. The man–machine mix and confidence in the robustness of the equipment stood out as critical to the growth of the regiment. That they now stood posted to 13AR, it was natural for the conversation to veer towards triskaidekaphobia. While some pretended that 13 meant nothing more than a number, many expressed that it was not auspicious. The majority view that developed was that it was unlucky, and some of them remarked, '*Hamari to kismet hi kharab hai,*' blaming their stars for it. This sentiment was voiced not only among the NCOs and JCOs but by many across all three classes. It was made worse when a few officers joined in paying heed to this superstition. It reached a critical phase when one of the SIC boys, named Wilson, made a more detrimental statement saying '*Ek to number 13 hai aur upar se equipment Vijayanta,*' suggesting that the number 13 and Vijayanta would both serve to be counterproductive. It was at this stage that Risaldar Santokh Singh, a Sikh JCO intervened and enlightened the others about the importance of number 13 as per Sikhism. He narrated the story of Guru Nanak Dev, the founder of Sikhism and the first of the ten Sikh gurus. He used to work in a store in Sultanpur Lodhi (modern-day Kapurthala, Punjab, India). Once when a customer came to buy wheat, Guru Nanak, who was deep in thought, weighed the grain by counting till 12 units of weight and went on reciting *terha* (meaning 13 in Gurmukhi) repeatedly.

But the word, a homophone, also meant 'yours'. So, when he would count to *tehra*, he would be reminded of how everything was *tera*, meaning God's. Guru Nanak would go on repeating, 'Everything is Yours, everything is Yours, Yours, Yours, Yours, *tera, tera, tera*.' In doing so, he kept doling out more than what was measured or paid for, but as per the folklore, the store would automatically replenish itself, confirming the belief that everything belonged to that One Supreme authority, the Almighty. This Grace of Almighty was symbolized by the persona of Guru Nanak Dev for the believers of the miracle. This version was quickly supported by other Sikh JCOs and the recently inducted Risaldar Major Gurbux Singh too. Thus, I had no hesitation in declaring *Tehra Sab Tera* to be espoused and enshrined in the regimental philosophy. This universal truth became the unofficial motto of the regiment and continues to be the cornerstone of its working philosophy. For the soldiering class, it sets the compass bearing professional excellence and devotion beyond the call of duty. I later learnt that the regimental *bania* (general store contractor) adopted this as his ultimate selling point and profited immensely by advertising '13 to a dozen' to market his goods and improve his turnover and profits.

Colonel M. A. Shah, one of the squadron commanders of 13 AR, recalls his experience as follows:

> Raising a new unit is no joke! There were no tanks and vehicles, no furniture, no kitchen items, nothing! All we had were officers, JCOs and men, and plenty of them! Almost everybody was disgruntled, which was only to be expected. When you are told to up sticks bag and baggage from your unit where you are comfortably settled and children going to a school, you are bound to be dis-jolly-well-gruntled!...
>
> The next best thing was to keep the men busy doing physical training. So, we had long PT periods and longer games periods!

Soon we knew each and every bump on the roads that ran past our regimental area and the inter-squadron games competitions began in right earnest, starting with football, volleyball and basketball and with the Battle Physical Efficiency Tests thrown in for good measure.

Visit of the COAS

General A. S. Vaidya, PVSM, AVSM, MVC & Bar COAS, was visiting the Mechanised Infantry Regimental Centre (MIRC) at Ahmednagar in early 1985. In honour of his visit, the MIRC Commandant Brigadier Desh Raj had invited all officers of the rank of Colonel and Commanding Officer in the station to his officers' mess. The MIRC Commandant's cocktail and dinner invitations had been received one day prior to the event. By now, Randhir was privy to my interaction with General Vaidya in Delhi, while I was on deputation with RAW. My anguish and disappointment was that the Chief, who was also the Colonel Commandant of 45 Cavalry, must have been aware of my transfer to 13 Armoured Regiment when I last met him in Delhi. If he had informed me, I could have exercised the option of joining RAW instead of facing the ignominy of being posted out from 45 Cavalry. I told Randhir before leaving for cocktails that I would meet the Chief and request him to visit 13 Armoured Regiment before returning to Delhi. He advised me against it as the regiment was still in its nascent stage, and such an arbitrary request may not have gone down well with the seniors. But I was unmoved and left after assigning responsibility to Randhir to have the unit in shipshape and ensure a high standard of turnout of officers/JCOs for the traditional line-up for visiting VIPs.

The cocktails started at the appointed time. The usual fanfare and drinks were flowing while the MIRC's jazz band played our favourite

Bollywood tunes. Having spent a few minutes with the MIRC officers, the general was now escorted by Lieutenant General G. S. Kler, who had taken over the reins of Commandant ACC&S. This was followed by the introduction and pleasantries being exchanged. Soon I was face to face with General Vaidya. Even as Lieutenant General Kler mentioned my appointment, General Vaidya addressed me, one hand still in the pocket and a whisky glass in the other.

> COAS: So, how is the new regiment?
> I sensed a note of sarcasm in the question thrown at me and responded, perhaps, a little aggressively.
> Me: 'Very good, Sir. 13 is a lucky number.'
> COAS: 'Oh, so you are taking the contrarian view! Don't you think you are also being superstitious?'
> Me: 'No, Sir. I have very good reasons for saying so, Sir.'
> COAS: 'And what makes it lucky for you?'
> Me: 'Sir, there are five reasons—13 AR is the only regiment in the annals of Indian military history with a class composition of Sikhs, Rajput and SIC; it is the first regiment being raised after a gap of 13 years, the last was in 1971; its raising signifies the revival of fixed class composition by the government; 13 may be the last regiment raised by a lieutenant colonel who was a war decorated officer of the 1971 war.'

The general heard me out patiently while other senior officers appeared a little jittery and nervous at my interface with him. 'So, you are the lucky one!' the general replied, and while saying so, he pulled out his hand from his pocket for a warm handshake.

The conversation soon steered towards the government's misguided manpower policy of 'All India, All Class' and General Vaidya's determined efforts to convince the government to revert to the earlier policy of a fixed class composition for combat arms.

The general spoke at length of his own war experience with the Deccan Horse and how a fixed class composition in the Indian context could become a battle-winning factor. Though nudged by Lieutenant General Kler not to breach protocol, I could not resist the temptation of requesting the COAS to visit the regiment before his departure from Ahmednagar. He confirmed the departure time with his Military Assistant (MA) and was gracious to accept my invite.

The COAS arrived the next morning, accompanied by Lieutenant General Kler, to meet all officers and JCOs of 13 Armoured Regiment. He questioned the RM on his appointment and the earlier regiment. He then spent time with the JCOs to receive confirmation that they were happier in a fixed class composition environment. He complimented the officers, and then turning towards Lieutenant General Kler, asked if there were any problems with the issuing of tanks and equipment to the new raising. I then escorted him to my ramshackle TRH office for a briefing on the progress made. He summoned his staff officer to bring the traditional COAS momento, to be presented to the regiment while expressing his happiness of visiting us. While escorting him into his staff vehicle, I thanked him for visiting and boosting the morale of troops. As he moved forward to enter the car, I quickly added, 'Sir, I told you that 13 is lucky.'

He broke into a smile and turning back said, 'What now?'

'Sir, lucky because we had the COAS as the first visitor to our regiment and also received our first memento.' He smiled and left.

The fact that General Vaidya was a fine and highly decorated soldier had a positive impact on the morale of troops. It was much later that I realized that he had personally selected me to raise 13 Armoured Regiment. Post Operation Blue Star, his individual assurance, patronage and advocacy of the fixed class composition had greatly influenced the government to reverse its 'All India, All Class' policy. That 13 Armoured Regiment was the first unit being raised after Operation Blue Star under the revised government policy with a unique class composition and comprised a squadron of Sikhs was a significant development to pacify the Sikh psyche. The intent had always been to foster brotherhood, and every attempt was made to further that goal.

As Colonel M. A. Shah, one of our squadron leaders, recalls:

> Time just flew by in Ahmednagar. Colonel Balram kept us as busy as he could, and very soon, the squadrons began to develop a spirit of their own. The South Indian squadron came into its own when the festivals of Onam and Pongal were celebrated, with all of us sitting together and eating scores of delicacies put on banana leaves! The squadrons went for a week each to the KK Ranges, where we camped. I had organized inter-troop map-reading and cooking competitions, which were enjoyed by one and all. I had some old, wise troop leaders—there was Nazar Singh in 2 Troop, Hardev in 3 Troop besides Tara Singh in Administrative Troop. I think that Kirpal, a tall, spirited Khalsa from 7 Cavalry was in 1 Troop. Surjit, a harmless, sweet chap was the senior JCO. The SHQ had some good NCOs who were thrilled when I accompanied them during the point-to-point marches! I drove a Vijayanta tank for the first time and was quite happy with the experience...
>
> Sometime in March 1985, the tank collection parties were sent to Kirkee under the Technical Officer with strict instructions to check the tanks, tools and associated equipment thoroughly before taking them over. Collection of A vehicles is a long, laborious process, and it would be months before they got back. In comparison, the collection of B vehicles (jeeps, 1-tons and 3-tons) is short and sweet, and I was one of the officers detailed by Balram to move to Bombay under the second-in-command, Major Randhir Singh. Randhir scandalized me—the man cannot speak a single sentence without at least two or three expletives thrown in! I honestly thought that there would be a mutiny

> when he spoke thus to the troops, but then slowly and gradually, everybody realized that those words were part and parcel of his 100-word vocabulary, so they let it pass. Our move to Bombay was by train. We stayed in the COD premises and came back by road to Ahmednagar in our brand new vehicles.

With the arrival of tanks and equipment, the trade and conversion training commenced in earnest. The officers and a few JCOs/NCOs from the Vijayanta regiments took on this important responsibility. The squadron's commanders and other officers were interacting with the men on a regular basis during PT, drill, games and conversion training. Each morning, a coordinating conference was held, where we shared the progress of the work done and set fresh tasks for the day. The officers were encouraged to speak their minds. The simple analogy was that as pillars of this new regiment, they must build the edifice of their own choosing. A determined effort was made to create a working environment within which each could contribute by being free, frank and fearless if the regiment was to become the first amongst its equals. The ideas and bold suggestions from this talented pool of officers turned into the biggest asset and blessing for the regiment. As the commandant, I realized that gradually each member had taken on their tasks with responsibility and was doing at their level what I was doing at the regimental level. This collective effort did not need a daily dose of motivation or direction but quick decisions for implementation. Individual initiative and solidarity amongst officers permeated down to the rank and file. It acted like a spark to ignite the creative potential at the squadron level where each individual reached out to excel and do better than the others.

During my meetings with the senior JCOs of the squadron individually, the untapped potential of the three classes would surface. While I sometimes received feedback from officers that I was driving them too hard, the response of these squadron sardars was virtually a demand for more resources, more passion, more competitiveness. Reflecting on this divergence and the varying responses between the officers and the senior JCOs of the squadron led to the realization that as sardars of their squadrons, they were privy to the true aspirations of their soldiers. Deep down, each individual was prepared to shed sweat, tears, even blood, for what he perceived to be a noble and worthwhile task because the intrinsic desire for excellence, success and glory was embedded within every soul. When the individual perceives the final objective as moral, upright and principled, it spreads fast amongst other members and becomes the collective aspiration of that group, which the squadron sardar cannot ignore while functioning within the squadron that has been organized on a single class composition. Born and brought up in the same environment, possibly the same or neighbouring village, with common friends and acquaintances, to finally return to the same environment, post retirement, his military reputation and contribution lives long after he has retired. This realization emboldens him to project this authenticity of group aspirations to his superiors, without fear or favour, once he is convinced that he will be heard. The overall impression I gathered during the early days was that there was great energy and dynamism amongst the troops at the squadron level. This potential had to be harnessed by setting high standards of excellence and competition. I was convinced that the difference between a good regiment and a bad one was not a matter of equipment or class composition but of human spirit. Mere enthusiasm was not enough, excitement was necessary. Beyond that fervour, controlled, trained and timely guidance must be provided. The officers, JCOs and NCOs, who I recognized as movers and shakers, could be given greater responsibility while maintaining a firm grip over their natural tendency to take liberties, also to keep a check on some of the angularities which had singled them out as problematic in their previous units.

Through it all, what kept me inspired was this phenomenal poem on my office table:

POLITICS
We move, the wheel must always move,
Nor always on the plain,
And if we move to such a goal
As Wisdom hopes to gain,
Then you that drive, and know your craft,
Will firmly hold the rein,
Nor lend an ear to random cries,
Or you may drive in vain;
For some cry 'Quick' and some cry 'Slow',
But, while the hills remain,
Uphill 'Too-slow' will need the whip,
Downhill 'Too-quick' the chain.
—Alfred Tennyson

A team of officers under the second-in-command and the adjutant took on the task of rewriting the SOP of the regiment. As Vijayanta regiments are similarly organized, the task amounted to modifying the SOPs that the officers had brought from their earlier regiments. No root and branch changes of the rules and procedures in operation in other Vijayanta regiments was visualized. With a few changes to meet our special needs, it would suffice and be reviewed subsequently. A lot of coordination was necessary as collection parties had to be despatched and periodic reports were to be submitted to different HQs. I appointed Captain Mantaj Singh as the adjutant to undertake the charge of all A and G subjects, which he handled with maturity.

As work progressed, word was received that the regiment would undergo an exercise with troops before it was declared fit for war, followed by an administrative inspection by the commandant of ACC&S. The allotment of the Annual Training Grant, Annual Contingency Grant and the Technical Training Grant provided funds to undertake the modification of a large number of vehicles, such as harbour trucks, rovers, cookhouses, shelters for RHQ offices and caravans, so that the unit could take to the field and deploy on mobilization. Similarly, funds allotted under the above were to be used for establishing regimental institutes and offices and for the procurement of targets for annual field firing. Proper planning and coordination took place under the 2IC, and the team of officers included Ravi Dhillon, Sayal and the EME officer. Officers exploited their regimental contacts and explored local offices and military establishments to add both in terms of ideas and resources.

Squadron Spirit

While the Sikhs and Rajputs coexisted in a number of regiments, working alongside the SIC squadron was a new experience for both sides. The differences manifested in all aspects of regimental life—language, food habits, competitions, inspections and parades. It was virtually a culture clash. It is different when you interact with a single or a small group as it would have been the experience for all. Now they had to contend with a composite group. Minor leg pulling by Sikhs, such as referring to the SIC as '*tambi*' (younger brother in Malayalam) in a slightly derogatory form, sometimes with a malicious tone or intent, was now being responded by the caustic retort of '*oye kake*' (Hey, brother in Punjabi) from the SIC. This was more manifest in the JCO mess, where all three classes had to dine and live together. Risaldar Pillai (ex 45 Cavalry) approached me a few days before Pongal in January 1985 with an invitation. I queried if the standard would be the same as in the previous regiment, where 66 per cent were SIC. Due to our long association, he mentioned that individual collection was low, since this was a new regiment. However, he wanted to use this opportunity to set an example that SIC were second to none. He requested that as his present commandant, I should provide some financial assistance for the Pongal celebration. I agreed on the assurance that the celebration would be of a high standard and good quality of food would be served. He left with a glint in his eye. I knew I had to prepare for fireworks, being aware of his 'talents' since the troop training days in 45 Cavalry.

The first festival in January 1985 was Pongal, which also happened to be a regimental holiday. All officers, JCOs and families were invited for the Pongal lunch by the SIC squadron. An elaborate traditional lunch was laid out. The entrance to the dining tent had been decorated with banana leaves and traditional motifs. The SIC wore traditional white shirts and *dhotis*. Most had a *tika* on their forehead, having completed puja before arriving at the lunch venue. The guests were seated in rows facing each other. Each one sat cross-legged on *durees* and mats. A large green banana leaf was laid out in front of every guest. The absence of spoons and forks was a clear signal to use bare hands to eat, as was custom. The menu carried a wide variety of preparations including rasam, vegetables, curd, chutney, *papadam* and a variety of sweetmeats. The aroma of food spread across the hall to mingle with the smell of agarbattis. For many Rajputs, Sikhs and some of the officers and families attending, this was the first Pongal meal that they had ever eaten. Somewhere in the middle of the meal, Risaldar Pillai walked up to confirm if the arrangements were satisfactory. He appeared happy with himself. In hushed tones he tried persuading me to prolong the meal a little. It was as though I had become part of some conspiracy. Sitting across were the burly Sikhs, who had come wearing fully starched clothes with ample spread of glue (fixo) to keep their untrimmed beards in place. In a separate row sat the Rajput JCOs, awaiting their first Pongal experience. The SIC dishes they were now consuming were not their regular bill of fare. As the lunch progressed, the extra dose of red hot chillies, procured from the south, began to hit their stomachs. In some cases, you could virtually see sweat drip from the forehead through the beard, falling pit-pat on the banana leaf. The profuse sweating spread through the garments and was cause of both mirth and embarrassment amongst the innocent victims, as was evident from their reaction. As is military custom, none could get up till the commandant finished his meal. Coming from an SIC regiment, I was in no hurry as the food was within my tolerance level. Some of the officers were in the same state as the Sikh JCOs. The dripping glue (fixo) and the sweat-covered plight lasted only a few uncomfortable minutes but got embedded in the memory of the regiment's brave hearts. The look of triumph and smile of satisfaction on Pillai's face and that of many other SIC did not go unnoticed. The Risaldar Major, himself a victim of this scam, reported the lunch as a 'chilli conspiracy' during his briefing to me the next morning. The trumpet of rivalry and competition had been sounded by the Rajputs as also the Sikhs. Their coming festivals would be celebrated at a grander scale with a 'surprise' as part of the package. The harmless ruse of the SIC had ignited the fire of reciprocal response from the other classes. The clever *tambi* had cast the first stone. The coming weeks and months would now witness an intense, spirited clash amongst the three squadrons to outperform each other. The proud Rajputs utilized Durga Puja to reclaim their pride, and the Sikhs waited till Guru Nanak Dev's birthday to hold a *guru ka langar* at a grandiose scale. Thus, every task given to a squadron became an opportunity to outshine the rest. This intense spirit of competition manifested in all spheres of regimental activity, be it games, inspections, parades, maintenance, including such mundane things as family welfare, family line inspection, *barakhanas*[1] and military manoeuvres. Their bonding, sense of glory, individual pride and intense comradeship was matchless.

As part of regimental routine, games were played compulsorily every four days in a week. A basketball cement court was created, and regular matches were conducted between officers and JCOs. It helped break the formality and rank consciousness of the military life. The regimental youngsters, having spotted an unused basketball post in the nearby church, convinced the priest to part with it. Mir and Mantaj, two ace golfers, roped me in to accept a challenging round of golf with the club members. A closely contested match ensued, finally ending up on the bar on the 19th hole, in which bottles of scotch and whisky drained out from our pockets. A makeshift field mess was established in the TRH using the Annual Contigency Grant (ACG). It served as a watering hole as also a meeting place for the families and a nebulous ladies club. Randhir and Sayal were two forced bachelors living in the mess, who took on the mantle of being the friend, philosopher and guide to all youngsters dining in the officers' mess. The customary dining in/out was not overlooked, and Mr Ajay Gupta and Mr Amardeep Singh enjoyed the spirited hospitality extended to young officers in a cavalry mess. Holi was celebrated with gusto and served as an ideal opportunity to revel, rejoice and let one's hair down. After the traditional gulal and *pichakaris* and warm embraces, the sherbet containing the intoxicating thandai took over, followed by wine, whisky, group dancing and singing along to the folksongs that many of us had learnt in our younger days. The mess staff and other onlookers would have looked shocked and horrified at the range of wisecracks and lurid songs sung by this gathering. Fortunately for

---

[1] A special meal for jawans, as part of a special event or celebration in which officers and JCOs also participate

us, most of them were also in a similar state of inebriation.

Welcome to a YO

A signal from MS branch provided the news of a youngster, A. S. Dhillon, joining the regiment direct from the Officer Training Academy (OTA), Madras, as a short service commissioned officer. During a late-night drinking bout with the merry bachelors of 13 AR and their mentors, Randhir and Sayal hatched a plot to welcome the new officer. Shail Jha, a youngster from Madhubani in Bihar was selected to play *sewadar* to A. S. Dhillon on arrival. It was a long night for the bachelors, who were having a rollicking time putting forward suggestions on how Shail should dress, the dialect he should speak, the questions he should ask. We had also suggested that he make some innocuous subtle personal enquires about his tastes and lifestyle, which may qualify him for a membership to the family of 13. Randhir was channelling the dialogue with full veto powers in his capacity as the senior-most forced bachelor living in the mess. Randhir, himself a particularly loveable raconteur, ably supported by other youngsters, had finalized the welcome plan to the tee. The innocent young officer on de-training on a Saturday morning was given an impressive reception at the railway station, before being escorted to his room, where the *sewadar* took charge. In a couple of hours, thanks to Shail's frequent visits to the officers' mess, the officers of the regiment knew more about A. S. Dhillon than his parents—an anxious group sat around Randhir and Sayal to debrief Shail and widen the scope of every new enquiry. The prank played out over the weekend and gave us a deep insight into the mental make-up and habits of the officer, while we were in splits for days because of how the drama had unfolded as each *dramatis personae* narrated his version. Much of what was known cannot be put to paper for military decorum is to be maintained. Those who are inquisitive may contact Shail, Yadav, Choudhary, Sengupta, Ajay and Randhir for finer details. Maybe Shail still retains the ₹10 note that he had received as tip for procuring a packet of Wills cigarette, which he had dutifully shared with his 'Troop Leader' *saab*.

Regimental Badge and Motto

Making the regimental badge involved the creative abilities of all members of the 13 fraternity, including the ladies. The core team sat down to determine the essential features of the larger cavalry fraternity, that had to be retained. A maze of entries was considered, some even coming from officers posted to ACC&S. The younger soldiers put up several entries, very few coming from the JCOs. My understanding was that young soldiers were better educated and more forthcoming and expressive. Teaching an old dog new tricks was anyway never easy. The discussions were long and endless. They varied from cobras and cougars till one fine day when my wife displayed rank badges of a captain used by her brother while he was Adjutant, PBG. Her suggestion to use the PBG star fired the imagination of all and became a unanimous choice. Research confirmed its usage by royalty as a sun sign. As this by itself would not pass the muster of AG's branch, AHQ, it was agreed that Shail Jha should prepare some sketches based on the following guidelines of the core team:

- Lance and pennant replica of 16 Light Cavalry, it being the oldest cavalry regiment, having SIC in its class composition
- The sun sign, a traditional symbol of the Suryavanshi Rajput. The 'sun burst' was being used to denote the rank of the officers serving in the PBG. The sun sign would carry an oval design,

as seen on the badge of 17 Poona Horse but embossed in the centre of the sunburst. Within the outer and inner perimeter of the oval would appear the motto of the regiment—*Veer Bhogya Vasundhara*. The writing would be in Hindi and would appear in the shape of an inverted horseshoe, a symbol of universal good luck and reminiscent of the cavalry heritage.

- The Arabic numeral 13, adorning the centre of the oval, which would be modified for resemblance with the equivalent Gurumukhi numeral. This task was taken over by Mantaj.
- Each half of the sun symbol, would carry 13 sun rays, both horizontally and vertically.
- The badge without the crossed lances and pennants would be used on the belt buckle and pouch and the collar dogs which were then in vogue (since discontinued) like the format adopted by 1 Horse (Skinner's Horse).
- The reverse side of the badge would carry the symbol of Hindu, Christian, Sikh and Muslim religions, with the inscription, 'unity in diversity'.
- The AG's Branch had issued orders against the use of bi-metal badges by newly-raised regiments. We pushed our case for acceptance as the sunburst had to appear in its natural, distinctive colour.
- Lastly, having turned down suggestions for the regimental motto received from the others, I explained the importance and relevance of *Veer Bhogya Vasundhara*, the loose translation being: 'The brave shall inherit the Earth'. This quote from the Bhagavad Gita applies to all Indians ready for the supreme sacrifice for the defence and honour of their country. I remember one of the majors quipped, 'Sir, is this also the motto of your former regiment?' I had replied in the affirmative—the Army chief had powers to change my regiment, but I have the choice to retain my

motto. Thus, *Veer Bhogya Vasundhara* became the motto of 13 AR.

- This badge was welcomed by both the troops and the families alike. A special *sainik sammelan* was held, and the design and significance of the badge were explained. We had extracted the salient features of the badges of famous armoured regiments like PBG, 16 Cavalry, 1 Horse (Skinner's Horse), 17 Poona Horse, 45 Cavalry, while retaining the lances, pennants and the horseshoe of traditional cavalry to weave together a unique design that was distinctive and appealing. As their commanding officer, I could see the radiance on their faces and a sense of pride. The response from all the three SIC, Rajput and Sikh squadrons was most gratifying. The badge of 13 Armoured Regiment carried within it the rich culture and tradition of the Indian cavalry while integrating the glory, heritage and sacrifices of its class composition, spread across numerous regiments, through unspecified battlefields across all ages. The motto taken from the Bhagavad Gita is the advice given by Lord Krishna to Arjun, reminding him that the earth is for the brave and that one needs to act fearlessly when duty calls. Under the traditional good luck charm of the inverted horseshoe, the power of 13 would radiate like the rays of the sun in all directions, to destroy the enemy who raises his head. A wave of cheer and enthusiasm found expression in the thunderous applause, unusual during *sainik sammelans*. Gradually, appreciation also came in from the personnel and families of other regiments stationed in Ahmednagar. Officers from outstations visiting the regiment would comment favourably on the bi-metal regimental badge on the black berets. Similarly, our own personnel returning from temporary duties would share comments and appreciation of our regimental badge as heard from other arms and services they had come in contact with. It soon took the form of *langar gup*, circulating within the larger mechanised fraternity, appreciating it at different forums. I had reason to be happy that while the first Pongal celebration had ignited the inter-squadron spirit, the badge and soon the flag would lay the foundation of the regimental spirit and become a mark of distinction and rallying point for the regimental officers, JCOs and ORs.

Regimental Flag

Before deciding on the flag, we put together miniature flags of all regiments in their regimental colours. Too much similarity existed in their colour and design, diluting the identity of the flag and the unit they represented. The thought that a flag must be distinctive and should reflect the mission orientation of the unit and its personnel alone would make it a genuine symbol and a rallying point of the regiment. The need to integrate colour, texture and shape to remind the personnel of the purpose and mission of the unit and its individuals was, in my view, of paramount importance. This was to become the cornerstone of our philosophy for designing the regimental flag. Days and weeks passed by in dialogue, research and contemplation until the day a mental image of what the flag should be evolved.

The realization that being an army unit, certain colours would be a taboo was accepted by all. The long association of the cavalry with certain colours was inescapable, which further limited our choice. Within this narrow band, the colours selected were the traditional ones of the cavalry—French grey and scarlet red. The design alone would give the flag an identity, which was fundamental and vital for every tankman. The very essence of armour warfare was crystallized into a simple concept—penetrate and destroy. The flag design would reflect the philosophy of 13 Armoured Regiment and simultaneously encapsulate the central dictum of tank warfare. We finally produced a design in which the tank-fired shell (scarlet red) would be shown penetrating the grey enemy armour to split it wide open after destruction. The cornerstone of the unit's philosophy, interpreted by each tankman, was that each one must remain focused and determined to penetrate and destroy the enemy's armour while remembering the basic training of '*ek gola, ek dishmun*'.

To add additional value and a sense of history, we reconnoitred the Bhingar area of Ahmednagar to track down the tailor who had tailored the flag of the erstwhile 13 Lancers, a regiment that had been gifted to Pakistan after partition, while retaining the Sikh squadron. On 16 March 1985, the flag was hoisted for the first time after invoking the blessings of the Almighty. The religious heads of the local temple, mosque, church and gurudwara were present to participate in the formal ceremony. A 'special order of the day' was published and sent to all personnel, explaining the relevance and importance of the flag as well as the strengths of the regiment. The essential theme was 'penetrate to destroy'. This was possible only by remembering that 'the daily work that you do is making the flag'. This does not stop when you leave the service or retire, as you could continue to help and work for all those who served with you and those who continue to serve the flag.

In these 37 years, though there have been changes in the class composition, colonels of the regiment, commandants, turnover of officers, JCOs and other ranks, yet each one plays out his destined role and makes his individual contribution to keep the flag flying high. The flag becomes the medium that keeps us connected and united.

Flag Hoisting

A flag hoisting ceremony was held at the TRH lines in Ahmednagar on 16 March 1985 where the commandant raised the flag for the first time. The ceremony was organized by the 2IC Major Randhir, and Captain Mantaj with the help of other officers and regimental personnel. Preparation of the ground, a concrete base for the flagpole, painting of the base in regimental colours, selecting the correct material for the flag, supervising the stitching, coordination of the religious ceremony, contacting the religious teachers and drilling the special guards of 1x6[2] selected persons was done without creating any waves. The sense of cooperation, dedication and commitment was truly praiseworthy. The effort spent in correcting the minute details in dress and deportment reflected the participant's planning and desire to excel. I have no hesitation in saying that the overall standard was in many ways better than that of a well-established regiment. After the ceremony, I submitted the 'special order of the day', published in the HQ Central Command magazine titled *Surya* in 1986, as an article on behalf of all officers of 13 Armoured Regiment. The same is placed below:

1. 16 March 1985 will go down in regimental history as the 'Scarlet and Grey Day', a day chosen to hoist the regimental flag for the first time. It now flies at the regimental quarter guard in a gleam of colours, reflecting our sense of honour and pride in 13 Armoured Regiment. Having invoked the blessings of the Almighty, we dedicate ourselves to the glory of the flag. The honour and prestige of the flag should never be compromised. For this we should be prepared to make the supreme sacrifice. Unwavering loyalty and total dedication alone can instil in us the courage necessary for this task.
2. The colour and design of the regimental flag have been chosen with care, so that it correctly reflects the unique aspects of the

[2] It is a military guard of one commander with six jawans, who are dressed in the ceremonial dress to raise/ lower the regimental flag at reveille and retreat.

regiment as also the potency and power commonly associated with the number 13. As you are aware, this is the first and only regiment in the annals of Indian military history with a class composition of the SIC, Sikhs and Rajputs. It also heralds the acceptance of the traditional fixed class composition for new raisings after more than a decade of raising mixed class regiments. Finally, with a spate of upgradation in ranks, it could well turn out to be the last AC regiment raised by a lieutenant colonel. History is replete with examples of the strong influence exerted by 13. The coming days will bear testimony to this universal belief. As Guru Nanak Dev has said, '*Tehra Sab Tera!*'

3. The scarlet and grey colours have been arranged to represent a tank-fired projectile penetrating steel. This expresses the unique character of 13 Armoured Regiment. The colours combine the traditional and the modern whereas the design highlights the basic motivation of the trained tank crew, penetration and destruction. The French grey is the colour of the cavalry and represents the elan and panache of the bygone generation of cavalry horsemen. The scarlet is the colour of the courageous and brave warriors—the colour a soldier sees while at the threshold of martyrdom. The warhead provides a sense of direction, drive and determination to reach the target and overwhelm it. In brief, the flag is the cornerstone of the regimental philosophy, wherein every individual must cultivate and hone the traditional soldierly virtues and gain excellence in his sphere of specialization so that at the selected point of decision, the combined might of every individual, crew, troop, subunit and unit can be delivered accurately and decisively.

4. As your commanding officer, I have selected the colours and designed the flag based on the unique character of our regiment—as also my perception of your strength and potential. While I have designed the flag, and Roonwal (an ex-tailor of 13 Lancers) has stitched it, neither of us can claim to have made the flag. Each

one of us, be it officers, JCOs, NCOs, ORs, miscellaneous categories, tradesmen, all have made the flag and will continue to do so every day of their lives in the regiment. Many of you must be saying, 'the only thing I have done since coming to 13 Armoured Regiment is guard duties, Battle Physical Efficiency Tests, working party, night parade, or conversion training. How could I have made the flag? Yes, you have made the flag because the work that you do is making the flag. The flag is your belief in yourself—your dream of what you want to become. The flag symbolizes your faith and courage. It is your battle of yesterday and the mistake of tomorrow. There will be times when you are strong and brave, weak or miserable, tired or heartbroken, hungry and lonely, sick or wounded, sometimes in pain, fear or danger. You will have to face all these situations and more in regimental life. Your thoughts, words and deeds, in short, the work that you do, unmindful of the circumstances or the nature of work, will be your contribution to making the flag. This contribution is not restricted to any rank, class, grade, trade but encompasses all. The flag cannot be more than what you believe it to be. The flag is all that you believe it to be. So, work hard, play hard and train hard. Keep your morale up and resolve firmly to perform your duty at all costs with full faith and dedication. On parade or off parade, it will be your duty to make a daily contribution in making the flag. Every good deed will strengthen it. Only then can it fly higher and reach the pinnacle of glory.

5. Regimental flags are not made in a day. It is a continuous process in which each one needs to contribute willingly and cheerfully. Remember the regimental philosophy and the unique character of your unit. Invest your belief in the scarlet and French grey flag because this flag cannot be more than what you believe it to be. To believe is to be strong. The work that you do is making the flag.

6. Make this a daily habit. Having raised the flag, it is now our

bounden duty to raise it higher so that it occupies a place of honour within the galaxy of the Armoured Corps. This calls for a lot of hard work, blood, sweat and tears. For the regimental flag we should be prepared to give all this and more.

7

A Regiment Fit for War

For a unit to be declared fit to fight, there are two mandatory conditions—inspection by the commandant of ACC&S and exercise with the troops. 13 AR had been earmarked to be placed on the orbat of 4 Infantry Division, forming part of 1 Corps. Colonel Baldev Singh, posted as Colonel General Staff, had issued a tentative date for the conduct of exercise at the K. K. Ranges, approximately 30 kilometres away from the location. The SOP on mobilization had been prepared, details of loads to be carried in A1, A2, B and F echelons had been worked out, and demonstrations were conducted. Tank crews and squadrons had fine-tuned their drills and appeared confident at having conducted their squadron training after the field firing.

A few days prior to the exercise, the Deputy Commandant Brigadier S. K. Sonpar, VrC, called me to discuss the conduct of this exercise with the troops. Brigadier Sonpar VrC was the squadron commander of the T-55 tank squadron (ex 63 Cavalry) placed under command 45 Cavalry during the 1971 war. Sonpar was a decorated soldier and had only recently been posted to Ahmednagar. We had met each other several times during briefings and recces. On the second day of the Battle of Garibpur, two troops of his squadron, along with his 21C Captain P. F. Kewalramani had been placed under my command. Some of his officers and men had been decorated for gallantry under me. We were meeting again after a gap of 13 years. As always, he welcomed me with open arms and narrated our war experiences to the exercise umpires, who had assembled for briefing. After the cup of tea, he shocked the team of umpires by announcing how he had seen my individual performance as well as that of my subunit during the 1971 war. For a war-experienced officer now commanding 13 Armoured Regiment, a test exercise by umpires who had never fired a shot at the enemy was neither necessary nor justified. It was his opinion that the test exercise should be declared a success without even conducting it—he felt that the exercise could at that very moment be declared as closed. Having said that, he winked at me, his face wearing an impish look, confident that the umpires would contest the decision. The reaction did not take long. A shocked chief umpire jumped out of his seat to say, with some seriousness, that he was to submit a written report of the exercise, a copy of which would be forwarded to 4 Infantry Division. His point was valid, and I supported it, thanking Sonpar for the faith expressed, adding that it would be helpful to me as a commandant to deploy the regiment and run through the exercise. Two days later we had successfully completed our first regimental exercise with troops mounted on Vijayanta, the best-known tank of the Third World.

The exercise was followed soon after by the annual administrative inspection. This needed careful preparation as a draft programme of inspection, along with a detailed brochure of A, G, Q account branches had to be submitted to the inspecting officer. A day before the inspection by the general officer, a battery of officers led by Colonel V. Shankar would descend on the regiment to inspect documents and prepare notes for the inspecting officer. On the day of inspection, the complete unit would undergo the BPET, followed by the introduction of officers and JCOs, briefing of the commandant and visit to the unit area and quarter guard. The inspecting officer could order the mobilization of the unit or set any task to satisfy himself on the organization, combat and administrative efficiency of the unit. Finally, a customary meal would be offered to him the same afternoon, or later, in the evening, subject to the progress of inspection. The general was a stickler for battle efficiency, physical fitness and fair play. The unsaid portion of the inspection was the responsibility shouldered by his appointment, wherein he was to initiate an Annual Confidential Report on the commanding officer and review reports of all officers of the regiment.

Prior to the inspection, Randhir met me and expressed grave concern about lunch being included in the draft inspection programme as the TRH was operating as a field mess and was unfit to offer a meal for the VIP visitor. I shared his concern but added that our brochure reflected the running of a field mess, which I would not deny. His other major concern was the BPET. He had made up his mind to report sick on the day of the inspection, as he would fail in the BPET. This would be a blow to his Rajput pride. Like me, he was a heavy smoker but not in good trim. I told him not to report sick as this would reflect poorly on his profile and would draw adverse comments from Lieutenant General Kler. It would be more pragmatic to appear in full uniform with the Field Service Marching Order (FSMO) and appear normal, leaving me to manage the problem.

On the day of inspection, Lieutenant General G. S. Kler arrived at the appointed time to see the full regiment on parade, ready for the BPET. Randhir, a little nervous, dressed in FSMO, brought the parade to *saavdhan* (attention) with his soldierly word of command and marched forward to hand over the parade to me, announcing at the same time the total number attending the parade. Before he could turn around to take his designated place, I winked, reassuring him that his interest would be taken care of. I brought the parade to attention once again as Lieutenant General Kler stepped up to receive the report. He spoke to the men briefly before checking with his staff officer about the manning of points along the 5 kilometre route as also the synchronization of watches. I handed over the regimental flag to him to start the BPET, adding that the regimental 2IC would keep him company.

A little surprised he said, 'As the CO, you need not take this test, instead accompany me.'

'Sir, this is a new raising; my leading the race will motivate others.'

As he nodded his head, I called out, 'Major Randhir, please fall out.'

As I advanced towards the start point, I could see a cheerful Randhir in a quick march. His day had been made.

I was a certified cross-country runner of the Academy in the NDA. During the Senior Command Course, I had become a fitness freak and had regained my physique and stamina. I was not only able to complete the BPET but was among the first dozen to cross the finishing line. The regiment was in fine fettle. Except for two in satisfactory grades, all others were in the 'excellent' or 'very good' category. The general shook my hand and complimented the regiment on its good performance.

The night before the inspection, the 'O' group had assembled in my house along with the regimental ladies. The dreaded lunch was on. This meeting was, in reality, crisis management of converting the field mess inside the ramshackle TRH fit for the VIP host. My wife took charge while the rest of the 'O' group sat silent, except Randhir, whose participation as the President Mess Committee (PMC) was inescapable. Jayshree had been made aware of the task assigned to Manbir and his wife, Binny. A rough draft menu had been worked out by the ladies. After a joint inspection of the mess by the ladies, the decor, wall hanging, curtains, carpets, crockery, seating arrangement, everything else including flowers, towels, toiletries, and every last detail had been earmarked. The entire exercise was carried out by the ladies, pooling in their resources and determination to show off the best TRH mess. The ladies put up a tremendous effort—from flower decorations, tablecloths, napkins, glassware, silverware, they left us all dazzled. Manbir's ability and talent to organize lunch by including three types of meat preparations and sweet dishes left the regimental ladies and officers licking their fingers. The last item on the list was the visitors' book, which had been hastily reclaimed and covered, in which Lieutenant General Kler paid glowing tributes to the quality of hospitality and mess get-up and food. Creativity, ingenuity, brotherhood, sisterhood and above all, the spirit of *Tehra Sab Tera* carried the day. The day was significant from another important point of view. Being a small town, the buzz of events spread like wildfire. The inspection by the general and the remarks he made became the talk of the town. The regimental officers and ladies were happy at the feedback they had received from local friends and acquaintances too. This permeated down to the rank and file and then took on a life of its own in the form of *langar gup,* which, with exaggerations, became grapevine for all those who encountered 13 AR. Everyone who learnt about the regiment during the period of its raising had a good word to say. This goodness didn't just escape into thin air. It rolled on and gained a momentum of its own, travelling by word of mouth to become one's spoken reputation and spread across to other regiments. This, along with one's badge and flag, became one's new identity. More than the good name, it gave each member of the regiment an intangible, exclusive aura that filled each individual's inner yearning for recognition that his contribution and hard work had helped in the making of the regiment, a satisfaction that money cannot buy, a deep sense of pride in one's identity and belonging.

With the raising now complete, it was time to reflect on the journey of the last few months and set a course for those who would join the regiment in the coming months. This was written to highlight the military traditions of our army, of which we were now proud members, having earned the tag of being fit for war. The corps, the teeth arm of the Army, had many unwritten codes of conduct and traditions weaved into its rich heritage. It was imperative to bring these to the officers' awareness, so it could become their second nature as they grew in the service. This was addressed to each officer by name in July 1985.

Guidelines for Officers

13 Armoured Regiment [S/US 0541056] raised vide AHQ letter no B/05431/Orgl(pers) (c) dated 11 December 1984 on WE 1011/1946/3 commenced raising on 21 December 1984 and has now been completed. With the regiment declared fit for war, it was essential to take stock of our collective and individual actions during the preceding six months. During this period, we had the opportunity to work, train and play together within the environment of 13 AR and determine for ourselves our strengths and weaknesses. As a commanding officer, it has been a gratifying experience to witness the ease and fluency with which all adjusted to their new regiment. This was, to a large extent, made possible by a conscious and sometimes unconscious acceptance of our military traditions, ensuring that in the coming days we would abide by these traditions. I put some of these down on paper to help increase our awareness. I was confident this would also help guide the latecomers as also the newcomers so that they would know what this team expected to make this a proud and resolute regiment.

Tradition of Public Service

The military life is devoted to public service, and the officer is a public servant. He goes where he is ordered to and performs the tasks which his duty requires. During peace he prepares himself and his subordinates for war. In war he leads his troops into battle. This might cost him his life. This is the military tradition.

Tradition of Avoiding Matters of Politics

The Armed Forces are the final bulwark for the preservation of the Constitution and the security of the nation. Loyalty to the nation and the elected government is traditional. While officers may agree to disagree in their own minds about policies announced by the Government, they do not have the right or privilege of public criticism of persons or policies which pertain to the Government of the nation.

Tradition of Achieving the Mission

This is the primary requirement of a military leader. The 'Army way' of undertaking a mission is to display enthusiasm, boldness and aggressiveness in getting the job done. Whether the task is tremendous in its scope of importance or a routine requirement, a pre-course cadre or any administrative or logistical responsibility, an officer is expected to complete it up to the desired standard and on time.

Tradition of Leadership

The officer is trained to lead from his earliest days. To do so, he must plan his work, assign missions to others, and ensure that the work is done skilfully and in cooperation with others. As the military leader will never rise high enough not to be responsible to others, he is trained to lead and also be led by others. The ability to develop teamwork and at the same time be a part of the team is, therefore, essential.

Tradition of Leadership

One of the most striking qualities required by an army officer is that he should be in a position of readiness to meet whatever tasks arise. Changes in orders, assigned tasks or duties are not the exceptions. The ability to accept and execute changes can be taken in stride if the officer retains the flexibility of mind and willingness to reach out for new ideas. This tradition includes physical readiness. In case one has flabby muscles, is overweight or needs medical attention, do take steps to get into good shape so that you are ready.

Tradition of Taking Good Care of ORs

Second only to accomplishing his mission, the officer's duty is to improve the moral, physical and intellectual quality of his men. The soldier remains the basic element of military strength. Therefore, an environment of decent, clean living, intolerant of vice, dissipation or flabbiness needs to be created. Officers must ensure that the personnel under their command receive thorough training, are in possession of individual and organizational equipment and receive good messing facilities and proper medical attention. In addition, proper religious guidance, recreation and advice to resolve personal problems should be made available. All men should receive fair and just treatment including spreading of the workload, gd/sentry duties, promotion and opportunity for appearing in tests and courses/cadres. The proper use of awards and punishments to ensure sound discipline, without the need for pampering is a must. Remember that proper care and attention to the welfare of men does not mean weakness.

Tradition of Selflessness

An officer is confronted constantly with putting someone, or something, ahead of his personal likes, dislikes or preferences. To ensure the good of the Army, the unit and the subunit takes preference always and every time.

Tradition of Discipline

The tradition of discipline is deeply ingrained into the mind and heart of every successful officer. The best way to develop it in the subunit is to set the example.

Tradition of Dependability

A good officer is one who gets things done. The most condemnatory weakness of an officer is the failure to complete the assigned task. Dependability extends to all things great and small. A dependable officer's word is taken for granted. His written reports and statements are accepted at their face value. He is trusted to discharge his responsibilities.

Tradition of Loyalty

An officer must be loyal to his men, his brother officers, his organization, his commander, the Army and the country. Suspicion of disloyalty destroys the usefulness of the officer. The commander can sense, or identify, a subordinate who lacks respect for him. Loyalty in the Army must go all the way, including contemporaries with whom one may be in competition.

Tradition of Cooperation

Cooperation is the art of working with others to attain a common goal. A staff officer or squadron officer needs to plan, coordinate and cooperate for the successful completion of any mission.

Tradition of Being a Gentleman

It is assumed that every officer is a gentleman. This must be manifest in his moral standards, conduct, appearance, manners and mannerisms as well as professional standards achieved in the performance of duty. It must be displayed in the things they avoid doing. Gentlemen avoid vulgarity. They do not drink to excess. They do not avoid payment of just bills or tender bad cheques. As a group, they enjoy the trust and confidence of the OR. We must ensure that as officers of 13 Armoured Regiment, we do nothing that will bring discredit to us individually or to the regiment.

The tradition of 13 will gradually evolve and emerge as a bright shining star over the Armoured Corps horizon. This star was born on 21 December 1984. It is now beginning to ascend, thanks to you.

8

Move to Kanpur

Prior to the completion of its raising, word had been received that 13 Armoured Regiment would be placed under the operational command of 4 Infantry Division located at Allahabad. The regiment would, however, be located at Kanpur and would come under the infantry brigade for local administration. The news brought cheer to the troops, as Kanpur suited the personnel of all three squadrons due to its connectivity to their hometowns by train and road. The troops who spend long periods of separation from their families can still bear difficulties if they can reach their near and dear ones quickly from their place of duty. A big industrial town with historical and ancient buildings or a tourist attraction mean much less to the troops and fade into insignificance if the station is well connected by road and rail. For some of the Rajput boys, it was a godsend as many belonged to the neighbouring town and villages. The Sikhs appreciated the proximity too. Even for the SIC, it was a popular military station as the train connectivity to their homes was very good. The delay and disappointment caused while switching two or three trains to reach home would be avoided. Advance parties despatched to Kanpur sent encouraging reports. However, available family accommodation for rank and file would be limited. This was a handicap that the men in uniform had got accustomed to as very few stations had accommodation as per the scales laid down by the government.

The Kanpur Cantonment was established in the year 1811 and is situated on the right bank of Ganga. It is bound by the Kanpur city area on the remaining three sides. It is the largest in India, both by area and population. The area of the cantonment is approximately 17 x 17 kilometres.

Kanpur (then spelt as Cawnpore) played a prominent role in India's First War of Independence in 1857. India witnessed one of the grimmest stories in the history of its independence on 27 June 1857 when around 300 British men, women and children were slaughtered at the Satti Chaura Ghat, later gaining the unsavoury reputation as the Massacre Ghat. Those who escaped their brutal fate that day were later killed at the Bibighar Massacre. The rebellion was believed to have been led by Nana Sahib Peshwa, after whom the ghat was renamed as the Nana Rao Ghat. Some of the oldest ordnance factories and depots, including a gun factory, are located here. The tourist attractions include St Patrick and St Mary's Church, Cawnpore Club, a golf course and the Lal Kurti cemetery. The airbase is located within the cantonment.

The last armoured regiment located at Kanpur was 16 Light Cavalry. The arrival of 13 Armoured Regiment after a gap of three decades was welcomed by the citizens. It was nostalgic for the elderly and brought back memories of their association with the cavalry unit. The younger generations were thrilled to watch the Vijayanta. The Kanpurwalas found it easier to refer to it as *chaingadi* (vehicles with large tracks). When the tanks were unloading from the railway rolling stock MBFU at the railway siding onto tank transporters for carriage to the unit area, it was breaking news for the local press.

The move from Ahmednagar to Kanpur was uneventful. The local Brigade Commander Brigadier M. M. Lakhera had arranged a warm reception and extended full support to help us settle in the new station. The advance party had taken over a large double storey wheeler barrack of British vintage for single-men accommodation. The stay arrangement for the JCO was a few kilometres away, within unit lines of another battalion's complex, causing inconvenience to members of both units. The RHQ complex was an empty barrack with a shed taken over from the bomb disposal unit still further away. The officers' mess was an old, dilapidated building on the banks of the Ganga, with no separate officers' accommodation for bachelors. No garages for A and B vehicles existed. My first meeting with the Station Commander Brigadier Kohli, Commandant, Central Ordnance Depot (COD), Kanpur made me realize that without the concurrence of this wily old ordnance officer, no improvement in the state of accommodation was possible. The stock reply that I received was that Kanpur was an approved Key Location Point (KLP) of the infantry brigade, whereas the armoured regiment was inducted as a transit unit. There was merit in this analogy because a KLP unit must be provided with its authorized scale. Linked with this was the emotional quotient that the infantry units had come from field areas and deserved priority. His pet phrase that 'poverty had to be shared' cut no ice with us, because the accommodation with peace establishment units under his administrative control as station commander was left unaddressed and was never taken into reckoning. The brigade commander tried to influence a favourable decision and even gave some additional sheds from his pool, but the station commander, whose channel of reporting was the Area HQ, remained unmoved.

Colonel Vinod Kochhar, OC Advance Party, recalls his experience:

> Till I reached Kanpur I had never realized that the infantry considered themselves superior to armour or vice versa, since the

> whole brigade was NOT willing to part with their holdings to accommodate the armoured regiment...
> They all decided to reappropriate a house next to the Ganges as the officers' mess for the regiment. Later on, I found out that this was done intentionally since no married officer used to accept this house as street dogs used to pull out the unidentified corpses dumped between the house and the Ganges waterline, up to the house verandah and eat it. A horrible scene!

While the regimental trains rolled in and the squadrons were allotted a share of what was available, I proceeded to the Division HQ to call on Major General Guddi Grewal, General Officer Commanding (GOC) 4 Infantry Division.

General Grewal was a popular officer in the Armoured Corps and carried a sterling reputation of being a large-hearted cavalry officer who stood out for his professionalism and qualities of head and heart. He had a cheerful demeanour and a ready smile on his otherwise inscrutable face. A few years ago, we were both posted in Ahmednagar and, as bachelors, dined in the same mess. He occupied the corner room in the same building block, generally reserved for the senior-most dining bachelor posted there. While we would sometimes meet during a hurried lunch, mostly it was when rushing out to make a dash to the golf course. His regular fourball of Colonel S. P. M. Tripathi, Colonel B. C. Joshi, Colonel R. Grover would sometimes have one absentee member caught up in some urgent work or out of station. A telecall from one of the colonels to join the fourball became a regular feature. In due course, Colonel Joshi got posted out to command an armoured brigade and I agreed to join the foursome. A few weeks later, Guddi Grewal was golfed out too. It was a wonderful experience being part of this fourball. The easy banter and recall of their escapades from the days in the academy, as young officers, or personal attributes of each other made each game an event to look forward to. Guddi appeared as the most informal one and easy going in lifestyle, but his golf game was sharp and his drives hard and long, much like his reputation. While I missed playing golf with him, his departure on posting got me the corner room along with the inglorious title of the senior-most bachelor. Now sitting face to face in his office, he shared in confidence that his posting to HQ West Command was on the anvil and would be announced shortly. He was aware of our accommodation difficulties at Kanpur but would accompany the Corps Commander Lieutenant General V. N. Sharma in the next few days to do his best.

A few days after my return, Randhir, while briefing me on the improvements carried out maintenance works started by the MES (Military Engineer Services), sprung a surprise. He mentioned that he had received a few calls from his acquaintances as well as one from the Station HQ, asking for a crate of rum. Randhir had turned down the request saying that our CSD-run canteen had not been established. The officer replied a little arrogantly that his request was for cheap liquor that the unit would have picked up while leaving Ahmednagar. Maharashtra's excise on liquor was much lower in those days than most other states, especially when compared to Uttar Pradesh. Some units moving from states in low excise areas invariably carried a huge stock of liquor in the railway covered wagons, later transported in military vehicles to be sold in the local market or units. The proceeds, sometimes pocketed by corrupt officers or deposited into regimental funds, were always open to misuse and audit objections. Newly raised units, short of funds, were known to have indulged in such a practice under the guise of garnishing their institutes and messes with air conditioners and silver. A few officers had approached the 2IC to mention this idea to me, which I had rejected outright. I had communicated to Randhir that I was aware of officers asking regimental couriers, returning from low excise states, especially the Northeast, to carry a few bottles of whisky for a function or mess party, but I always discouraged this. This subject was then raised by another officer during a regular meeting. It appeared to be supported, especially by officers arriving from regiments raised post-independence. The final decision was that a soldier and an officer were authorized to carry their two-month entitlement while proceeding on annual leave, as per army orders. As their commanding officer, I would take responsibility for this decision and authorize each officer, JCO and OR to carry the same. The regiment would not carry any liquor stock, and existing stock of the canteen could be sold to applicants before departure from Ahmednagar. Randhir's assurance and acknowledgement that the direction had been carried out in word and spirit were sufficient. He now confirmed that no excess stock was carried. The request took a more devious turn when a few days later, a senior JCO informed Risaldar Major Gurbux Singh that some personnel of the field security section attached to the Station HQ had made discreet inquiries from regimental personnel regarding the availability of cheap liquor in the regiment. Other personnel may have been questioned by these covert intelligence operators, trying to unearth concealed liquor stock, but it was not brought to my notice. Having drawn a complete blank, they must have made their report to the superior authority. A few weeks later, the officer commanding the field security section attached with the Division HQs, who was on a visit to Kanpur, took time off to call on me in the office. He confided that a letter from the Station HQ had set the cat amongst the pigeons, but all attempts to establish the veracity of the report had failed. He had made a report of this to the divisional staff as well as the station commander. This single decision not to fall victim to the lure of liquor and create unauthorized funds saved us from making administrative and professional compromises; it also created a clean and healthy environment within the unit.

The physical dispersion of accommodation spread over nearly

8 kilometres was an area of concern as cohesion and supervision within the squadron and regiment was affected. To circumvent this, a duty JCO roster at the squadron level was prepared, so that contact and communication with troops was maintained. Army vehicles to transport personnel for parades and games were authorized for troops. Inclement weather, pollution, the density of traffic on the cantonment roads due to proximity to civil areas necessitated this concession as an inescapable need. Limited accommodation for the families of NCOs and JCOs could only be overcome by applying for Compensation in Lieu of Quarters (CILQ). This was granted to individuals as cash in lieu of hiring accommodation in civil areas. This too was calculated against the overall percentage of accommodation authorized to the entitled ranks. Compensation was an appropriate word but brought no succour, as individuals had to shell out money from their own meagre resources in a class 'A' city where rents were sky-high. The practical implication of high rent translated into substandard accommodation in unhygienic areas and longer distances from the place of duty. The difficulties of the ORs were in many ways unsurmountable and demanded empathy. Concessions in terms of parade attendance, provision of transport, leisure hours and a total ban on work parties on Sundays and holidays became the unwritten order. Military exigencies overlooked this, but the rank and file took this in their stride as part of the regimental ethos.

The state of office accommodation and lack of garages for A and B vehicles was a challenge. It reminded me of my younger days when 45 Cavalry moved from Babina to Bagrakote in West Bengal. A couple of thatched huts within an open patch adjoining tea gardens greeted us on arrival. A gravelled track from the main road led to the unit area. In the absence of regular accommodation, the tents and field latrines were the only shelters provided for men. The officers' mess was a rundown shanty made of three small barracks with tin roofs and walls lined with asbestos sheets. Bathrooms had to be erected in tents, and Indian-style commodes were used, as no piped-water or washbasins had been provisioned. It appeared to be a crying shame that a regiment carrying crores worth of military equipment had to stay where the basic infrastructure for the troops was not available. The way the unit overcame problems of military negligence and inclement weather became an early military lesson that 'when the going gets tough, the tough get going'. I shared these thoughts with the other officers and senior junior commissioned officers (SJCOs), individually encouraging each of them to exploit the environment. The unclaimed resources of station units, parachute factory, central ordnance depots, ordnance equipment factory and even the Air Force base in the close vicinity became our hunting grounds. Furniture, tarpaulins, salvage items, paints, parachutes, Corrugated Galvanized Iron (CGI) sheets and the woodwork would be all up for grabs to meet the immediate needs. The 'loot' began to arrive in driblets. The Sikh squadron appeared more adept at this transgression while the Rajputs, initially hesitant, followed with enthusiasm. The SIC was to handle it more low-key and be discreet but effective. My own office, a standalone storeroom with a ramshackle bathroom attached, covering an area of 16 x 14 feet, had a perforated tin roof. Just across the main road was a barrack, housing the quarter guard in one half and all the RHQ officers crowded into the rest. Though never comfortable, we were able to become functional, notwithstanding the shortfalls. At around the same time, a signal, followed by a telecall, announced the visit of the Corps Commander 1 Corps accompanied by the GOC 4 Infantry Division to the regiment.

Monsoon had set in, and the sight of dark rain-bearing clouds left us wondering if the helicopter carrying the corps commander would land. The morning held out but was followed by torrential rain by the time the introduction of officers and JCOs had been completed. Randhir needed no introduction as Lieutenant General V. N. Sharma, Corps Commander, recognized him as an officer who had served under him when he commanded 66 Armoured Regiment. As is customary, no officer complained of shortages or mentioned the difficulties he had overcome, as problem-solving is a function of command and leadership. This was to be adequately covered by the Risaldar Major and the SJCOs. Within minutes of the commencement of the formal briefing in my overcrowded office, heavy rains lashed out as if a storm had broken out with full ferocity. The tarpaulin that had been secured over the tin roof, ripped off, making an eerie sound. Before my briefing reached the halfway mark, raindrops from the porous roof were all over the table. General Grewal turned around to address Brigadier Kohli and half-jokingly said, ' The Armour boys don't appear very happy!' Keeping the bad weather and a leaking roof in mind, General Grewal signalled me to end my briefing. A light drizzle continued even as the corps commander insisted on visiting the unit lines. The Risaldar Major had arranged for a few umbrellas as the VIP group walked towards the quarter guard, avoiding the puddles of water en route. Unmindful of the weather and the ground conditions, he visited the lines and the ancillary buildings. Walking through the lines, I made a few suggestions of how, by readjustments, my requirement of additional accommodation could be met. Brigadier Kohli had considered these suggestions earlier too, but they had been dropped when objected by the other unit commander. Brigadier Kohli maintained the view that a shortage of accommodation existed in the station and 'poverty must be shared by all'. Brigadier Lakhera acquiesced by maintaining silence. Before leaving, Lieutenant General V. N. Sharma turned around to address Kohli and Lakhera by making a cryptic observation, 'poverty is evident, sharing is not'. The visit of 13 Armoured Regiment was over as Brigadier Lakhera accosted the corps commander to the brigade headquarters.

'Come and see me soon,' said Guddi Grewal to me as he departed.

A few days later, I met him in the office as he was soon to relinquish command. Before leaving, he presented a beautiful silver pen holder to the regiment to be placed on the visitors' table in the officers' mess.

The arrival of a new Division Commander Major General K. C. Tewari and Corps Commander Lieutenant General Y. S. Tomar heralded the end of the monsoon and the start of a collective training phase of the regiment. This was important for a newly raised regiment to integrate with the other formations and units of the formations. Squadrons would be affiliated with brigades to carry out infantry tank cooperation and marry up for allotted operational tasks. This entailed the close appreciation and understanding of formation tasks as well as a comprehensive understanding of drills and battle procedures to be adopted. Initially, the squadron commanders were encouraged to meet with their brigade commanders, HQ staff and unit commanders, followed by chalking out a joint training programme and conducting a mini exercise with the battalions wherever possible. The squadron commanders would form part of the Brigade 'O' group, and units of other arms and services would be placed under its command or be affiliated for specific tasks or for a specified time. The squadron commander had to perform the task of an adviser to the brigade commander. He was expected to have a good working knowledge of other arms and services. He was encouraged to be frank and forthwith in his advice and ensure that the task set for his subunit was within the technical parameters of our equipment and in consonance with the principles of employment of armour. On completion of the brigade-level training, the regiment would get deployed in the exercise area to conduct training that was specific to the Armoured Corps and practice tasks likely to be assigned to an armoured regiment. The Corps Headquarter had planned Shakti Vallabh as a test exercise for 4 Infantry Division as many of the formations and units had been deployed in Punjab when Operation Blue Star had been in progress. The four-day exercise ran its full course with a bevy of umpires and briefings against a controlled exercise enemy to relearn lessons it had learnt in the previous years. The most active and energetic participant, in my view, were the Artillery Air Operation pilots, transporting an energetic corps commander, sauntering from one brigade to another in his chopper and landing in unprepared helipads to ascertain the veracity of locations given out through radio messages and the deployment of units. The debrief at the end of the exercise had spelt out no new tactical concept nor added any fresh wisdom to the many who had participated.

In the words of Colonel M. A. Shah (extracted from his written reminiscences of service in 13 Armoured Regiment):

> Sometime in mid-1986, we went for a field firing to Babina. I was detailed by the CO to take the B vehicle convoy to Babina via Jhansi. En route to Jhansi, one of our Shaktimans had an accident, and I had a harrowing time recovering the vehicle and taking it for repairs to a workshop in Jhansi! The two EME boys, who were slightly injured, were put in the hospital and then sent on leave by me. Major General K. C. Tewari , GOC 4 Infantry Division, was coming to witness our firing standards. So, Balram left no stone unturned in preparing for the event. Everything was spit and polish and geru, and there was tension in the air... It is amazing the things that a regiment worth of men has to go through for the naukri of one man! Also, after the field firing got over, we all went for a recce of the prospective training area and in a jonga-accident one of our NCOs, who had come with me from 73 by the name of L. D. Ram Singh, died.
>
> After the field firing got over, we went into squadron blobs for the collective training in the vicinity of the Babina Ranges itself. It was an enjoyable experience, having inter-troop cross country and cooking competitions! I also took the opportunity to go to Talbehat, which was nearby. I went to Sukwan Dukwan too. We

did our gun-cleaning there itself so that we would not have to face any problem in this regard after reaching Kanpur. The 105 millimetre is a wonderful tank gun, very accurate and penetrating. However, from the driving and maintenance side, the Vijayanta left a lot to be desired. The poor tank drivers were the most hard-pressed and unhappy lot!

1986 was a very busy year for me in Kanpur. There were inspections, exercises, inter-squadron games and competitions and most painfully, numerous trips to Allahabad (Division HQ) for sand-models and such-like events. The collective training, season that year was held from April to the end of May 1986 in the area around Kanpur itself. During this training, Balram came over to my squadron and very coolly took away Shail Jha as his IO! In the main exercise, we had to form a bridgehead over the Kooch Malanga Nala, and everyone used to talk about this bally *nala* in hushed tones. In actual fact, it turned out to be a piddly little *nala,* and my five tanks (one for each troop) managed to cross it without any difficulty. On the way back to Kanpur, I was bringing the B vehicles back in a convoy when, to my horror, I saw the vehicles weaving left and right on the road. Quite obviously, the drivers were fast asleep! In spite of Balram's orders to be back in Kanpur before first light, I took a command decision, halted the vehicles on the left side of the road and told the men to go to sleep. We started at seven the next morning and reached our lines in Kanpur safe and sound.

Once, Balram decided to have football matches between officers, JCOs and NCOs and the teams were made of three categories. The JCOs lost to both officers and NCOs. So, the final match was played between the winner teams. The final match between officers and NCOs stretched into extra time as there was no score. Even though it began to rain heavily, the match carried on as per Balram's directions till yours truly scored the winning goal!

9

First Anniversary

With December fast approaching, the regiment came to the consensus that the first anniversary must be celebrated grandly. It had been a hectic year of raising, as we were working hard to gain the status of 'fit for war', moving to our KLP location followed by the Exercise Shakti Vallabh, returning the hospitality extended to us by the Station HQ units and the units of the local brigade. There were many others, like the military hospital, supply depot, the EME and signal personnel attached to the unit, as well as station workshops and MoD units located in Kanpur. The division staff had developed a close affiliation with the unit and were always helpful to our officers visiting Allahabad. It was more an occasion of thanksgiving to our troops and their families for their loyalty and hard work. A special meeting was held in the officers' mess to chalk out the events to be held and assign responsibilities that would best utilize the individual talents among our officers, families and troops.

I had decided that I would remain an observer and would go with the programme based on the consensus, but I would retain my veto rights. All suggestions were welcome, and the ladies had taken the lead. The meeting had soon turned into a mess party, with the ladies and officers in animated discussions. With the wine and whisky flowing, the grey cells of the youngsters were running riot. The PMC and Mess Secretary prepared a draft programme that stood approved; no veto powers had to be exercised.

What 13 Armoured Regiment did during the three-day festivities was beyond my imagination. It started with a prayer meeting in the newly established mandir and gurudwara. Both had been adequately furnished. The prayer went beyond a simple recitation by the pandit and granthi. The participation of those present and attending the singing of bhajans and shlokas and the energetic rendering of aarti and ardaas left a telling mark. Many of those attending had made donations in cash or kind, thus adding a new dimension to the proceedings. This was followed by a *sainik sammelan* and a JCO mess lunch. The JCOs, attired in jackets and blazers and wearing the regimental tie or cravat, interacted with the officers in a friendly and dignified manner. Instead of ganging up around the commandant, as is the practice in most units, and nodding their heads in unison, they appeared more confident and self-assured to interact on a one-to-one basis. I had reason to be pleased with this happy development. We had done a few things to improve the JCO mess, but more would follow. The Pagal Gymkhana was a showstopper, for which participants from local units were also invited. The creativity, innovation and imagination of the participants, and the games, rides and jugglery on display were extravagant. While some appeared dressed as mythological characters from the Ramayana and Mahabharata, others came as Nihangs[1]. Some were dressed as Rajput warriors and snake charmers; one had even come as a leper sitting on a push-cart, seeking alms. His make-up and dress were so

[1] An armed Sikh warrior of the Khalsa army of the Guru that has been around for over 400 years

realistic that his entry sent the regimental police in a tizzy. Many in the audience were guessing the identity. The children of the JCOs and ORs were not far behind in adding colour and class to the proceedings. It was an overwhelming show where we ran out of prizes and had to announce cash rewards while the crowds cheered. Apart from the annual day celebration, the rivalry and competitive veneer had set into the squadron psyche as well. The bhangra party, colourful and loud, had ensured the participation of many from among the audience, while the SIC, dressed like a Pied Piper and a one-man band playing multiple instruments, had led the children dressed in colourful clothes to dance to his tune past the enthralled audience.

As the officers' mess had still not been fully furnished, the venue was shifted to the local DSOI. The complex was centrally located and provided easy access to visitors. It also had adequate parking. The venue enabled our creative team of young officers and ladies to innovate arrangements within the complex with a well-manicured lawn and large rooms. The PMC decided to outsource the catering to a well-established local eatery. This pragmatic decision took the load off the mess committee. The DSOI management had laid some restrictions on party decorations inside the main lounge and the adjoining room as well as on the rearranging of the furniture. Hence, the earlier plans of using this room as a dance floor on the evening of 21 December were now discarded. This problem was quickly overcome by the officers and ladies, who converted the empty swimming pool into an attractive psychedelic dance hall and requisitioned the ACC&S band. The existing gap between the pool and the DSOI veranda was covered by a *shamiana* to keep the cold out. The caterer was instructed to bring *sigris* for heating, and the layout of his dinner tables inside the *shamiana* would give the event a regal touch.

While the use of the swimming pool as a dance floor was acknowledged as a rare novelty, what struck a note of amazement amongst the invitees was the special effort of the regimental ladies to embellish the outer tent with sarees of all hues and colours. The special effects and lighting were, in the words of an infantry officer, 'simply mesmerizing'. Major General K. C. Tewari and his wife, both reluctant dancers, were persuaded to take the floor. Amazed by the energy on the floor, they decided to stay on. Credit is due in large measure to the Velvette Fog, the dance band of ACC&S, which had been arranged for this function.

The two liquor and soft drink bars inside the DSOI, and one closer to the entrance, kept the guests in good cheer. The veranda had a few chairs laid out for the parents and elderly guests not wanting to use the lounge. Once the band took a break, it was time for Mir Ahmed Shah to take over as the Master of Ceremonies (MC), with his smooth flowing voice. His rendition of old favourite songs appealed to the elderly, especially the all-time English favourite House of Bamboo and Be-Bop-A-Lula. He then got off the stage impromptu to invite Mrs Sweety Lal, a talented young lady, who entertained everyone with her lilting Bollywood songs sung in a mellifluous, honeyed voice. She was already in dialogue with the agent of a local music recording company who had spotted her budding talent. An impromptu Bharatnatyam dance recital by Mrs Kamal Choudhry, a newly arrived bride, had the audience enthralled. The MC, under some persuasion from the PMC, announced dinner. A lavish spread of vegetarian and non-vegetarian select dishes, tastefully spread out on the tables laid out in the *shamiana*, creating the desired ambience. The candles, flower arrangements and the now glowing *sigri* added to the ambience. In the background, the Velvette Fog band leader turned his craft into an artistic high to nourish the soul. Those not dancing were busy satisfying the human desire for appetizing food. Amongst the few civilian senior citizens was one doctor, a leading medical specialist, who, while sharing his reminiscences with the general, was overheard saying that the mirth and joy experienced at the party took him back to the year 1954, when another cavalry unit was located in Kanpur. Old timers who were present shared memories of the joy and happiness and thanked the PMC and other members profusely before departing. Finally, it was time for the regimental brave hearts and ladies to let their hair down and have fun till the wee hours the next day. Unknown to all was the surprise that Randhir had sprung when he announced that along with the dinner, he had ordered the next day's breakfast as well!

A break from the military routine was not going to last long. Just a few days later, the troops were out yet again; it was time for military ceremonials. The two immediate commitments before us were to despatch tanks to Delhi for the annual Army Day Parade on 15 January, followed by the Republic Day parade on 26 January. The other less-strenuous but equally important commitment was the demand for tanks for the 26 January parade being organized by 4 Infantry Division at Allahabad, where the Governor of Uttar Pradesh would take the salute. After due deliberation, I decided to give the responsibility of the parade at Delhi to the Sikh Squadron Commander Major M. A. Shah (later Colonel) and the one at Allahabad to the Rajput squadron. The SIC squadron would be called upon to give the residents of Kanpur, especially the school and college students, demonstrations and tank joy rides as part of Republic Day celebrations. The presence of Sikh troops under the command of M. A. Shah, a Muslim officer, would strike the right chord amongst the people of Delhi after the unfortunate event of Operation Blue Star in Delhi, where many lives had been lost. The international media, which had widely covered the Sikh riots, would register this message from 13 Armoured Regiment. The Rajput squadron was earmarked for Allahabad, as many serving personnel belonged to Uttar Pradesh, particularly, the district Allahabad. The TV coverage of the Allahabad parade would be shown on Doordarshan as the Uttar Pradesh Governor was the Chief Guest.

This would be welcomed by the Rajput squadron, especially their families—ever since our arrival in Kanpur, many officers—both serving as well as retired, along with civilians, including some members of the Cawnpore Club and Golf Club, had approached me to take a closer look and try for a possible ride on the Vijayanta. Every time tanks were sighted by school children and street urchins, the cry of *chaingadi* would rent the air. Since the Republic Day was a national holiday, we placed a few tanks and crews in the open field near our location so that the locals could crowd around for closer inspection. It was an appropriate day to help them satisfy their curiosity and also experience the thrill of riding a tank. Tea, biscuits and cold drinks were also offered as a public relations activity to win the hearts of the locals.

I cannot recall a dull moment during the entire period of commanding 13 Armoured Regiment. Perhaps it is true for most other commanding officers as well, but raising a regiment is a unique experience. If you learn to enjoy every new challenge and have the unstinted support of your team, rarely will you be overwhelmed by the immensity of the task. I was blessed with a positive outlook and had identified the movers and shakers among the officers, JCOs and men—the men who had the natural talent to lead. The regiments which sent the initial manpower, never realized that many among those they happily discarded as undesirable or disciplinary cases were, in reality, gems whose talent and potential was tapped by this regiment, and their invaluable contribution was utilized for the foundation, growth and emerging reputation of 13 Armoured Regiment.

10

Brass and Brasstacks

Planning

As Lieutenant General P. N. Hoon, then Army Commander HQ Western Command, recalls:

> In 1986, I attended a high-level secret conference, where the Chief of Army Staff General Sundarji was present, and it was decided to call the top senior officers and commanders to discuss the various contingencies that the Indian Army could face vis-à-vis the threat from Pakistan and how formation commanders should react from time to time to such a situation. This was necessary as new equipment was being inducted into the Indian Army, and it was important to update the Army's workings and theories in war. It was also important to hold such discussions and exercises in the event of a war. It was, therefore, decided at this conference that Operation Brasstacks would be conducted in four phases. Brasstacks I was a theoretical war-game exercise. It was to be

> conducted on the map to ascertain the threats India could face and from which directions. This was held in early 1986 in New Delhi for three to four days, where senior military commanders discussed how we could effectively engage in an actual war situation. These discussions were attended by then Prime Minister Rajiv Gandhi, and the then Minister of State for Defence Arun Singh, in the initial briefing.
>
> After this, Brasstacks II was conducted at the Western Army Headquarters at Chandimandir. Officers up to the rank of divisional commanders (major generals) were required to attend this second part of the exercise. There were sand model discussions of similar war situations that could develop at a lower formation level and discussions held about what actions would be initiated at that time.
>
> Brasstacks III was the next series in which all lessons that were learnt in Brasstacks I and II would be reduced in writing for updating our operational plans.
>
> The final was Brasstacks IV, which was to be held on the western border's desert areas, with troops actually participating with weaponry, tanks, guns and full-scales of ammunition in which the 'war wastage reserves were also to be activated, and total mobilization was ordered.

Brasstacks IV involved physical movement, during which the troops were actually mobilized for the implementation of the planned exercise, focusing on the desert region of Rajasthan. The plan was to test new operational concepts, particularly the mechanised infantry formations which had especially been raised for the desert flatlands of the Rajasthan–Sindh sector. Other objectives of the exercise included providing senior commanders with an experience in coordinating operations at multi-corps formation levels and testing new communications. Brasstacks was the largest military manoeuvre in modern Indian history. By the end of December 1986, two armoured divisions, one mechanised division, a host of infantry divisions, independent armoured, and infantry brigades were deployed approximately 100 kilometres from the Pakistani border in Rajasthan.

As Lieutenant General P. N. Hoon described it:

> It was peacetime when suddenly the Indian Army began moving from the east, south and the north to the west. They moved in trains, civilian aircrafts and convoys. No Indian saw a military movement at such a large scale and of this nature. It could only be a preparation for war. The media and the opposition parties had, at that time, blamed Rajiv Gandhi, the Prime Minister, for yet another blunder, as they had stated that he wanted to "divert public attention from Bofors to this war hysteria".

Operation Sledgehammer: Pakistan's Response to the Crisis

The Pakistani leadership felt an air of suspicion growing around this activity and viewed it as a plan aimed at bifurcating Pakistan. Pakistan's perception of Exercise Brasstacks created doubts that this was a military threat, and it went into a spin. The Army Reserve South (ARS) of 1 Armoured and 37 Infantry Divisions stayed in exercise areas, and this was extended instead of returning to Multan. A few weeks later, news came in about how Pakistan's ARS formation had crossed the Sutlej around Bahawalnagar, moved into the Minchinabad Salient and was assembling perilously closer to the Indian cities of Abohar and Fazilka. Similarly, the Army Reserve North (ARN) of 6 Armoured and 17 Infantry Divisions were relocated closer to the India-Pakistan International Border, to the area between the Chenab and Ravi rivers. In early December, the ARN was moved closer to the cities of Gujranwala and Sialkot. Both the southern and northern reserve forces were augmented with additional elements drawn from 11 and 12 Corps. The simultaneous movements into the Minchinabad and Shakargarh salients enabled Pakistan to initiate a two-pronged pincer attack in Punjab to cut off Kashmir from the rest of India. Unfortunately, the hotlines between the two Director Generals Military Operations (DGMOs) were not functional, leading to misunderstandings on the nature and purpose of Exercise Brasstacks.

Mounting Tension

The first instance when India explicitly acknowledged its awareness of developments within the Pakistani borders was in mid-January 1987. The then Indian Prime Minister Rajiv Gandhi and his Army Chief General Krishnaswamy Sundarji publicly drew attention to Pakistan's deployments. General Sundarji also disclosed that additional ammunition stocks were being issued to Pakistani forces. Civilians had been evacuated from certain frontier towns in Pakistan, and a curfew had been imposed in others. These actions were reported as causing considerable anxiety in New Delhi. As far as the Indian Army was concerned, General Sundarji informed that except for the units in the Brasstacks area, the Army was placed at usual locations. 'We are trying to get in touch with Pakistan and others to see what the problem is.' He claimed that such a provocative action from Islamabad was not a consequence of the Indian military Exercise Brasstacks.

General P. N. Hoon, GOC-in-C Western Command shares:

> It was 15 January 1987 when I was required to be present in New

> Delhi on the occasion of Army Day. That evening, there was a reception given by Sundarji at the Army House. The President of India, the Prime Minister and the Defence Minister were all invited. Whenever Rajiv saw me, he would walk up to chat with me. Even at this Army Day reception, when Rajiv saw me, he walked up to me and asked, "How is the Western Front?" I was sure that Sundarji had briefed him. I was having a cup of tea, and Rajiv had a samosa in his hand. I clicked my heels and told him, "Mr Prime Minister, Sir, the Indian Army is in fine fettle and very soon we shall be past our battle stations." To this Rajiv immediately reacted and asked me what I was saying. I repeated what I had just said. This was because the Pakistan Army's General Headquarters (GHQ) Reserves, North and South, were in the process of moving into their battle locations. This was an expected move, and I said that the planning and deployments that had gone into it would be obvious as Pakistan would be provoked. The greatest provocation that would strike the match was the deployment of the Indian troops in positions which would lead Pakistan to believe that India was about to attack. Rajiv was totally aghast and visibly angered with what I had just told him. He called for the Defence Secretary S. K. Bhatnagar and Foreign Secretary Venkateshwaran. They got into a huddle, spoke to each other and soon thereafter, Rajiv left the party; I had already scooted and asked my staff to organize my helicopter to Rajasthan.

The relocation of Pakistan GHQ reserves, mentioned above, led to the Indian army being placed on high alert, and the redeployment of troops under Operation Trident was undertaken. Reinforcements to Punjab from the Brasstacks exercise area, as well as from other parts of the country had commenced. The Air Force was also placed on operational alert and ordered to move its squadrons to forward bases in order to forestall pre-emptive attacks.

On 23 January 1987, Indian mobilization was made public. Pakistan's Ambassador was summoned to the Ministry of Foreign Affairs in New Delhi. He was told that if his government did not withdraw its forces along the Punjab border within the next 24 hours, India would occupy positions along the border in Kashmir and Rajasthan.

Operation Trident

The east-west deployment of troops for Brasstacks was changed to north-south while the troops were on the move due to Operation Trident and the swing in the conduct of Exercise Brasstacks. General Hoon's description provides a rare insight:

> I told him (Chief) that the entire Indian Army, with all its might, was moving towards the Western Front, and there is no button that I could push to stop this movement immediately. It will take at least 10–12 days to halt the forward movement and another 10 days to rearrange the concentration. I asked Sundarji what had happened, but the latter did not reply. Instead, he asked me if the number of days could be reduced any further. I told him that if a whistle was blown now, even then it would take approximately six days and nights to stop everyone in their tracks and another two to three days to rearrange the plans. This would mean at least 10–15 days.

Exercise Brasstacks was stymied by Pakistan when the Army Reserve South was moved across the Lodhran Bridge from south of Sutlej River to the north to locate itself opposite Bathinda and Ferozepur in the second week of January 1987. This deployment was within the overnight reach of Khemkaran, Gurdaspur, Amritsar, forming a pincer along with Army Reserve North to capture the salients in Jammu and Punjab. Soon after the Minister of State for Defence Arun Singh briefed the press, another briefing was organized by General Sundarji, highlighting the aims of Exercise Brasstacks and the Pakistani misperception and response. On 20 January, the Foreign Secretary A. P. Venkateshwaran was removed unceremoniously. A cabinet committee meeting on political affairs was called on 22 January for briefing by the Service Chiefs. This storm in the teacup electrified the political, diplomatic, military and media in the country and began to draw attention of world capitals. This is best reflected by the string of meetings that followed on 23 January with the Minister of State for External Affairs Natwar Singh meeting his Pakistani counterpart Akbar Humayun Khan. Shri N. D. Tewari and Arun Singh were engaged in a discussion with the Russian and American ambassadors respectively while our ambassador in Pakistan, Shri S. K. Singh was in dialogue with the Pakistani Foreign Secretary A. G. Noorani. Media reports of then Deputy Director of CIA, Robert Gates's visit to Pakistan reflected the prevailing tension and war hysteria in the subcontinent. A little before, Kuldeep Nayyar had dropped a bombshell, quoting the nuclear scientist Dr A. R. Khan that Pakistan had enough plutonium and know-how to make a crude nuclear bomb, taking tensions to another level. The appointment of V. P. Singh as Defence Minister by Rajiv Gandhi ended his effort to clip the wings of then Minister of State Arun Singh, even as the country announced Operation Trident to counter the Pakistani move under Operation Sledgehammer and movement of their Army reserves. The Pakistani perception of Exercise Brasstacks that it was India's politico-military objective to detach Sindh province and destroy Pakistan's nascent nuclear facility or straighten the Line of Control in J&K appears to have dominated the thoughts of Pakistani generals.

Negotiations began on 31 January 1987. The threat of war hung heavy across the border. On 4 February 1987, a reciprocal withdrawal of forces along the northern segments of the border was announced with both sides pledging to exercise 'maximum restraint and to avoid all provocative actions'. They also agreed to immediately deactivate forward airfields and lower the operational readiness of their naval forces. Tensions diminished in March 1987, with an agreement by the two nations to withdraw troops in the Kashmir area, followed by a second agreement to withdraw more troops in the desert area.

The truth of Brasstacks remains an enigma, as compelling events like Operation Pawan in Sri Lanka, the air crash resulting in the death of President Zia-ul-Haq and the assassination of Rajiv Gandhi diverted media's attention. Some military commentators like Ravi Rikhye, author of *The Fourth Round*, are reported to have said that India had missed a great opportunity in 1987.

For us in 13 Armoured Regiment, these developments at the national level escaped us completely as we were preparing to move by special trains to reach our training areas in the desert and reorient our squadrons/ troops to form part of the RAPID formation. The veracity of claims made by GOC-in-C of Western Command, the misinformation spread by the media as well as the political developments within the country were unknown to us as we were deployed for training in the sand dunes of Rajasthan, impervious to external influences due to the radio silence imposed during conversion training.

Media reports sparked widespread speculations and rumours of an imminent outbreak of hostilities between Pakistan and India. In Pakistan's view, India's failure to share timely and adequate information about its multi-service exercise, Brasstacks, not only violated an informal agreement which both sides had reached in 1984 (under which both countries were to notify each other in advance of any exercises taking place unusually close to the shared

International Border) but also served to reinforce suspicions regarding India's intentions. The unparalleled military activism lent credence that India was engaged in a military adventure as per accusations made by Pakistan. Some observers believed that General Sundarji, with an eye on Pakistan's advancing nuclear programme, was motivated by the preventive war logic.

Position of troops in mid-December

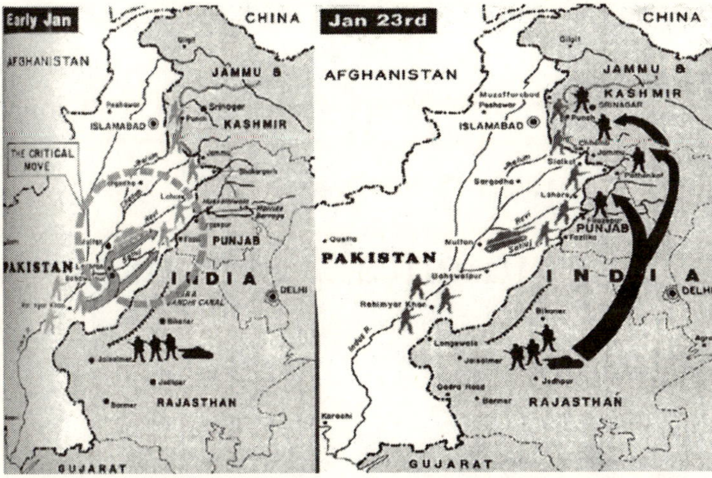

Position of troops in early January (left) and late January (right)

Troops start to pull out in February

11

Regimental Response

Warning Order – Brasstacks

Three days prior to Republic Day, an urgent telephone call was received from Brigadier Shankar Roychowdhury, BGS Intelligence at Central Command, who shared confidential information that 16 and 23 Armoured Brigades, earmarked to constitute Mechanised Brigades of 14 and 23 Strike RAPIDs had been withdrawn from Exercise Brasstacks due to unspecified reasons; he added that two other regiments had been earmarked to replace them—one amongst them was 13 AR. The same evening, a despatch rider brought a signal for me at the basketball court, where a match between officers and JCOs was in progress. While the game continued uninterrupted, I read the contents. It confirmed Roychowdhury's message, putting the regiment on a 72-hour notice to participate in Exercise Brasstacks. As per the regiment training programme, all squadrons were to conduct a night parade from 2000 hours onwards. 'B' and 'C' Squadrons had limited manpower, as the tank crews were away to participate in the Republic Day parade. After the game finished, I asked all officers present to assemble in the officers' mess after the commencement of the night parade for an urgent conference. During the day I had studied the regimental brochure and had clarified a few doubts from the staff officers regarding our major equipment shortages, so that I was prepared for the evening meeting. I had prepared my own list of operational deficiencies, which came in handy for the meeting in the evening.

When the contents of the signal and my conversation with Brigadier Roychowdhury were explained, a sense of awe and shock overtook all officers. Everybody had heard about Brasstacks, India's biggest exercise, in which virtually all armoured formations were participating. The scale was mind-boggling. So far, we had been viewing it from the sidelines, so participation at such short notice appeared like a cruel joke. It was both shocking and incomprehensible how a newly raised unit with no training in the desert was required to switch over for deployment with Strike RAPID formation. It demanded monumental effort, a reorientation on working in a Strike RAPID formation, training of crews in the desert, specially navigation, revision of certain SOPs as also changes in organization and manpower. It was a tall order and demanded a complete overhaul of the regiment. The unstated portion of fear was the rumour circulating in the media that the Pakistani response to the exercise could lead to confrontation. Most were certain that Pakistan would mobilize troops, leading either to a showdown or an extended deployment in the desert, ending in a stalemate.

It was good that the meeting was being held in the mess. A round of drinks was ordered to calm the frayed nerves. I shared a thought with them over a drink, a thought that I believed to be true: 'And if the trumpet gives an uncertain sound, Who shall prepare himself for battle?'[1] I was frank and openly admitted to

[1]A Biblical aphorism

the immensity of the problem that our inductionwould bring. The regiment had not operated in the desert and was not aware of the Strike RAPID concepts. Navigation in the desert without a GPS (Global Positioning System) or a gyrocompass was extremely risky—that said, the Vijayanta had neither. This would become a Herculean task, especially with the Vijayanta and the drivers, who had had no opportunity to drive over sand dunes so far. However, a small window of opportunity did exist, which we could build on, if as officers and leaders we exploited the talent and potential of those few who had come from the Vijayanta regiments and had operated in the desert. We could build a core team around the nucleus and then build on our capacity to take the challenge head-on. I made it clear that all doubts needed to be buried before we left the mess. As officers, we should project Brasstacks like a godsend and not a problem to our commands. Gradually the doubts and reservations began to settle down and the suspense and shock of the signal got ingested. Another round of drinks was ordered before we started listing our problems, shortages and major deficiencies.

The immediate task ahead of us was to prepare a comprehensive list of shortages and project the same to HQ 4 Infantry Division and Corps HQ. Over the next few hours, everybody got busy in an earnest preparation of lists with Randhir and Ravi Dhillon. Somewhere midway, Keju Yadav, the technical officer, threw a bombshell saying the tanks and vehicles would have to be painted in disruptive colours for deployment in the desert. His quick estimate added up to thousands of litres of paint. Shashank, who had been performing the duties of a regimental signal officer, highlighted the deficiency in the radio equipment. Virender pointed out another critical requirement—the gun pull-back apparatus required for the calibration of guns. While we were digging into the war equipment tables (WET) and the war establishment of the regiment, the Quartermaster Captain Sayal walked in, holding a fresh operation immediate signal instructing us to requisition rolling stock. By now, the mess had turned into a war-room, and the head clerk and typist sat in the adjoining bachelor room, preparing signals for despatch. Butalia brought up the subject of navigation in the desert. While other tanks had gyrocompasses, the Vijayanta had no navigation aid. Travelling limited distances in the plains and using the compass prismatic by the trained tank troop personnel could be managed. Using the compass prismatic across the barren landscape of the desert over long distances and multiple obstacles sent a shudder down everyone's spine. After listening to the doubts of many, Lieutenant Debu Sengupta threw a googly that floored all present. He had been a member of a civil flying club before joining the Army. The small flying club aircrafts had the compass 4GB fitted for navigation. This equipment was also in use by the Air Force. He could confirm its availability through a friend posted at the Air Force station, Kanpur. As per Debu, due to its small size and stabilization, it could be fitted onto a tank easily. Kanpur had the Air Maintenance Command located next door, which was overhauling and servicing all types of IAF aircrafts. The idea had an appeal and the practical application appeared feasible. He was asked to explore the availability. The list of needs kept multiplying till Randhir announced, with a little desperation in his voice, that we were touching the 150 mark. Of course, each item did not fall under the 'critical' head but a lesson of history was recalled by the now happy Ajay Arora, 'For want of a needle, a kingdom was lost.' This spurred those assembled to continue identifying non-critical deficiencies too. This idea received a fresh infusion from the QuartermasterCaptain Sayal, who quickly explained that in his experience of over 38 years in the Army, it was an ideal opportunity to get all deficiencies released from ordnance depots, since a ban on the issue from reserve stocks is permitted when mobilization is announced. The old campaigner, Sayal, knew that when there is tension prevailing on the border the demands materialize in double-quick time. This opened the floodgates of wants, and soon the list expanded to even include items that we had rarely heard of.

Peacetime restrictions on the movement of vehicles involved written sanctions from higher HQs, without which the traffic check posts established by local brigade and Division HQ would curtail the movement of the unit vehicles. Only the regiment had been placed on a 72-hour notice and not the complete 4 Infantry Division. The peacetime restrictions had not been lifted and continued to dominate the mindset of the regimental officers. So, when Keju Yadav brought a signal asking for a road move sanction of 3x3 ton vehicles for COD Allahabad, I looked surprised. This was a good opportunity to change the thought process of the officers. In an effort, made more dramatic for full impact, I tore up the papers and threw them in the air. I scrutinized the room and then spoke with a roar, 'You are now on war footing! You have 72 hours. When I assign you a task move on and complete it quick. No more signals need to be forwarded to higher HQs requesting sanctions for the move of personnel or transport. The peacetime restrictions stand waived!' My words jolted the officers and sobered up some of them. It was as if the cloud of doubts and restrictions under which army life is governed during peacetime had been removed, to reveal a new reality where the task and mission would gain primacy.

'Sir, but what if I cannot get this large demand of paint from Allahabad on which we have placed our indents?' retorted Keju Yadav, still doubtful of the orders that had been passed.

'You have my sanction to take the vehicles wherever paint is available. I want it before we load up for moving to the desert.'

'And in case we get delayed?'

'Obviously, I expect you to drive straight up to our detraining station—Suratgarh.'

It is to the credit of the training imparted to armoured officers and the agility with which they operate that all suspicion and reservations were dropped; what followed was the do-or-die spirit to electrify the personnel and prepare them for what was to come next.

In one sitting lasting nearly five hours, Randhir and Ravi Dhillon had tabulated a list with nearly 271 items required by the subunits of the regiment. The list contained both the operational as well as deficient items authorized on the war equipment tables of the regiment. The military establishment wanted the newly raised regiment to operationally deploy in the desert. Hence, there was the need to reflect complete WET deficiencies, along with manpower deficiencies applicable when so deployed. It was well past midnight when the 'one for the road' was ordered by the PMC. My job as the CO was done, and the directions were given. More importantly, the meeting was to convey to the troops that their officers were raring to go and take part in this major exercise. Secondly, it would also help break the mental barrier of officers conditioned by peacetime restrictions. This was a transition from peace to mobilization for war.

I remember returning home very late to catch some sleep. I was to catch a train to meet Mir Ahmed and the personnel participating in the Republic Day parade at Delhi at the crack of dawn. I was later told that hours after my departure, the GOC 1 Corps, Lieutenant General Tomar had arrived in Kanpur by helicopter, ostensibly to brief the Commandant 13 Armoured Regiment on the preparation for the new task. After I returned from Delhi, Randhir gave me a complete brief of what had transpired and his personal encounter with the corps commander. Around midday, Major Randhir received a cryptic telephone message from a duty officer that the Commandant 13 Armoured Regiment should be present at the Kanpur helipad for a briefing by the GOC 1 Corps. Randhir armed himself with the handwritten list of 271 deficiencies, listed the night before, having correctly appreciated the likely purpose of the 'briefing'. The general, whose love for the black beret was a subject of intense interest at his

Mathura HQ, alighted from the helicopter to express surprise at the presence of a Major Randhir. 'Where the hell is your commanding officer? Does he know that the regiment has been inducted for Brasstacks? Are you aware of your critical deficiencies?'

Randhir, fully prepared for the onslaught, pulled out his handwritten list of 271 items and explained its genesis during the night—'Prepared by "my commandant" the night before', he said as he handed over the list.

The General briefly glanced through it, mumbled something incoherent, before returning the same with a terse comment, 'Send a copy to my HQ', before he departed. That was the last we saw of the corps commander.

After the Delhi Republic Day parade, I met Major M. A. Shah and complimented him for the excellent parade. Over lunch he shared an illuminating observation relating to 13 Armoured Regiment's participation in the Army Day parade a few days earlier and his first brush with General Sundarji:

> We rehearsed moving six tanks past the saluting base in the Army Parade Ground a couple of times before the actual event. On 15 January 1987, my tanks rolled steadily past and I saluted General Sundarji with gusto. Second Lieutenant Ajay Gupta's tank did not lower its gun in salute to the COAS, as the gunner was annoyed at Ajay giving him a very hard kick as signal for lowering the gun. General Sundarji mentioned this in a lighthearted manner during the tea party thrown for the participants after the event: 'Hey, Major! One of your tanks refused to salute me!' He had observed this and remembered to point it out in a pleasant tone, half-smiling at my embarrassment, for the mistake made by a young officer.

I first met General Sundarji in 1968 when he was colonel. He had been brought in from Staff College, Wellington, as the chief instructor to conduct the Eastern Command Short Staff Course at Shillong. He created a lively impact on the students with his knowledge, wit and air of supreme confidence.

On taking over as COAS, General Sundarji had sent out a letter to all serving officers, which sent a wave of positive hope and promise of change in the thinking and working of the Army. There was a sense of excitement among the younger officers, but, I dare say, there were critical voices among the star ranks, who felt that it was uncalled for and populist. His efforts to inject fresh western concepts into the tradition-bound Army were criticized but never questioned. His biggest contribution was to lay the foundation for change and encourage the younger generation of officers to at least apply their own thinking and experience in all spheres of military activity.

My elder brother Lieutenant General Shamsher Mehta, then colonel, was the military adviser to General Sundarji. I remember asking him once, 'What makes Sundarji different from other generals?' His prompt reply was, 'He is a thinking general. While most others are reflecting on a new concept or proposal, he will be the first to share his thoughts and ideas fearlessly. Once done he will sit back and listen intently to the criticism patiently. The truth is that very few make a contribution to improve on the thought shared by him; most people only criticize and state of why it cannot be done.'

Journalist Shekhar Gupta has described General Sundarji as 'one of the most dashing chiefs, shifting the entire outlook and doctrine from defensive to offensive, attack-and-halt to assault-and-keep-moving, terrestrial to airborne, pedestrian to mechanised', No other chief has left behind such an abiding doctrinal legacy in India's history. He recounts how, as a defence reporter, not knowing that 25-pounder guns could be used in the direct fire mode, he kept wondering how brilliant the artillery gunners were that hardly any round strayed into the crowded locality surrounding the Golden Temple during Operation Blue Star. Many soldiers pointed out that the 25-pounder guns were capable of both direct and indirect fire but none did as rudely and colourfully as Sundarji.

'Ha! You defence reporters! You can't even tell the difference between bore and calibre.' And then, turning the knife even as he laughed, enjoying his own joke, 'You can surely be big bores despite having low calibre.'

Young officers of the regiment stood out as excellent examples of enthusiasm once they understood their task and were granted the liberty to execute without interference. For instance, when Keju Yadav realized that the critical gun pull-back apparatus was deficient and the tanks had to be repainted in the specified disruptive colours authorized for desert units, he moved his 3x3 ton vehicles to COD Cheoki near Allahabad. As the demand for paint was large, he was directed to another COD in Rajasthan. Having collected the entire demand and the gun pull-back apparatus from another ordnance depot, he arrived directly at the detraining station of the new unit location in the desert. The decisions taken during the conference in the officers' mess had galvanized the officers. It served as a small shock wave that changed the mindset of overregulated, disciplined regimental officers. The realization that a unit placed on operation alert must shed peacetime restrictions shook up each one of them—they now knew this was no routine meeting and that, henceforth, we would be working in this new operational environment. Similarly, Debu Sengupta visited the local Air Force station to ascertain the availability of the 4GB compass used on aircrafts to understand the mechanics of fitting the same on a Vijayanta tank. Our good relations with the local Air Force station had earlier helped us airlift regimental officers from Kanpur to Delhi to attend Shashank Yadav's wedding. I visited the Air Force base to meet the airbase commander for the acquisition of this 4GB compass, which resulted in immediate release, on loan, removed from a grounded aircraft. By now, the special trains for moving the tanks had been marshalled at the Kanpur Railway

Station. The Air Force station commander, on learning that the 4GB compass was to be installed on the commandant's tank while the military special train was on the move, directed his technician to travel on the special train and stay till the completion of the task. The QM Sayal along with Ravi Dhillon took this opportunity to collect sleeping bags and tents for the recce troop that were not listed under the WET stores from the ordnance equipment factory. Other officers and staff virtually raided the local ordnance depots to collect all sundry items that could be put to some use in the desert. Similar actions were undertaken at Delhi, where the balance tanks sent for the Republic Day parade were painted in the desert's disruptive colour by the local workshops. Mir Ahmed, along with all his officers participating in the Republic Day parade, could never have imagined that they would be mobilized and moved straight into the desert. It speaks volumes of the resilience of our soldiers and also the strong bond of communication and understanding that exists at the unit and subunit level. As the commanding officer, I was more than satisfied with the initiative and response of not only the officers but also the JCOs and NCOs based on their earlier service experience. In the absence of specific orders, they undertook various actions to prepare themselves and their crew to reach a battle-ready state.

Training for Trident

I reported to HQ 36 Infantry Division, but a week later I was ordered to report to GOC 14 Infantry Division and then deployed in the desert. This was due to major policy change at the AHQ level as large-scale deployment in the desert had led to tension between the two countries. Due to Pakistan's aggressive deployments of Army Reserve South (ARS) and Army Reserve North (ARN), India responded to Pakistan's warlike posture under Operation Sledgehammer by reorganizing troops deployed under Operation

Trident to counter the threat posed. Formation commanders were understandably stressed due to the twin demands of Exercise Brasstacks now superimposed by Operation Trident. My meeting with General Pillai, GOC 14 Strike RAPID (14 Infantry Division) turned out to be a memorable one.

The general appeared busy drafting a letter when I entered his office.

General Pillai: 'Ah, new raising—13 Armoured Regiment?'

Me: 'Yes, Sir.'

General Pillai: 'Have you trained in the desert?'

Me: 'No, Sir. New raising.'

General Pillai: 'Vijayanta tanks? Any navigation equipment fitted?'

Me: 'No, Sir. None.'

I was still standing when he asked these questions. I felt he was being rude. Such basic questions should have been brought to his notice by his staff. That he had not offered me a chair or extended basic courtesies befitting a regimental commander reporting arrival to his formation was unexpected. Was it an act of arrogance? Irritated, I repeated my answers to his questions.

'Sir, you are right, 13 is a new raising. We have not trained in the desert, and the Vijayanta tank does not have any navigation equipment.'

No sooner had I finished the sentence that he retorted, a little exasperated, 'I suggest you report to my Colonel General Staff. We will see how to use your regiment.'

I was in full control, but also a little hot under the collar. I had taken umbrage at his last statement, also because he had interrupted me while I was still talking.

'Sir, you need to ask me one more question—what is the spirit of this regiment?'

He looked up, a little astounded at this unusual question. The realization that the draft that he was writing might have to wait

> a little longer troubled him. He looked into my eyes, giving the impression that he would have to suffer this dialogue a little longer.
> 'So, you tell me,' came his quick rejoinder.
> My reply hit him hard. 'I have an excellent bunch of officers with a matchless spirit best exemplified by their ingenuity. They are well aware of their limitation—the absence of navigation equipment and prior experience with the desert. As you may be aware, the 4GB is a compass used by light aircrafts of the Air Force for navigation. My boys procured and had it fitted on to my tank while we were in transit from Kanpur by the special military train. I will lead the regiment, which will lead your division. Why don't you come and witness the trial tomorrow evening?'

The reply and the tone in which it was delivered made him push the draft further away. He must have sensed the anger and hurt as well as the challenge I had delivered. He now requested me to sit down, called in Colonel A. S. Rao (later Lieutenant General), who was the Colonel General Staff, and offered some tea and biscuits. The meeting lasted longer than an hour between the GOC and his armour commander, with Colonel A. S. Rao dutifully taking notes. In my experience, in every battle of life as also in the affairs of the everyday, there comes an opportunity, sometimes a very fleeting one, which can turn the tide in your favour, with you winning the day. This was my opportunity. I fired my salvo without fear or reluctance.

The impression I gained was that for some reason the general had developed a negative mindset towards the Armoured Corps. Rumour had it that this division had come under severe criticism during an exercise conducted by the Corps HQ a few weeks earlier. The integral Mechanised Brigade had been pulled out for deployment in Punjab under Operation Trident immediately after this exercise. The role of the Mechanised Brigade would now be performed by the HQ of an infantry brigade, under which the integral armoured regiment of the division plus the newly inducted 13 Armoured Regiment would be grouped along with other elements. Lieutenant General Hanut had ordered a fresh training exercise for the division along with the reorganized Mechanised Brigade prior to the commencement of Exercise Brasstacks. Due to changes in the ORBAT of 14 RAPID, an element of apprehension and nervousness existed within the Division Headquarters on the outcome of the proposed exercise. To make matters worse, the division commander was reported to have suffered a mild stroke during the last exercise but was fit to continue in command. I came to know of most of this from the commandant 48 Armoured Regiment (Integral Regiment) much later.

A little more relaxed and attentive, I now offered him the alternative to help my Vijayanta tanks navigate in the desert. I explained to him that my previous regiment had discarded their PT-76 tanks, which had a semi-gyrocompass fitted. This equipment was still fitted on the decommissioned tanks and held with the Central Armoured Fighting Vehicles Depot (CAFVD), Kirkee. The suggestion had been that instead of the single 4GB compass, he could help get a squadron worth of these semi-gyrocompasses which I would fit onto my Vijayanta tanks. The idea appealed to him instantly. A brief explanation of the working of the semi-gyro, its accuracy and fitment convinced him of its utility. By now his excitement was evident as Colonel A. S. Rao was nodding his head in agreement with his boss. The GOC knew the commandant CAFVD personally, having attended the National Defence College together a couple of years ago. He lifted the receiver of his hotline and booked a lightning call to Kirkee. After a few quick pleasantries, he made a bid for 15 semi-gyro compasses. The officer confirmed that the decommissioned PT-76 tanks were available in his depot, but it would need approval from the AHQ along with some time for the removal of the semi-gyros from the tanks. The excitement was palpable. He quickly put the line on hold to share with me the response that he had received. I suggested that

I only needed his 'yes' for the removal of the semi-gyro, which would be returned after Exercise Brasstacks ended. He repeated the same to the commandant CAFVD as he punched the connect button. 'Okay, okay, so that is done, wonderful. I will send a DO letter with my request. It will be with you in 24 hours, thank you.'

There had been a radical shift in the mood of the GOC. A fresh round of tea was ordered while he dictated his letter to the PA. Meanwhile, Colonel A. S. Rao arranged for a courier to leave the same day. I requested the GOC to book a call to Ahmednagar for me to speak with my regimental officer, Captain Manbir Singh, posted to ACC&S. I quickly explained to Manbir the recent developments and asked him to put a dozen regimental personnel together to travel to CAFVD Kirkee, remove 15 semi-gyros and despatch them to the regiment on priority. All he said was 'WILCO', giving all the assurance that was needed. It was a tall order for a captain to marshal men and transport, travel, remove, pack and despatch the semi-gyros. It stands out as a good example of what regimental officers are capable of when tasked to perform an act in regimental interest.

The DO letter for the commandant CAFVD, requesting the cannibalization of the semi-gyros by 13 Armoured Regiment, was ready and handed over to the waiting courier, who was to deliver the same to the commandant CAFVD. The GOC now asked a few questions about the regiment and its raising. He was unaware that the regiment had marshalled from three different stations to concentrate in the desert for Exercise Brasstacks. I explained to him about our unique class composition. I then requested to provide me seven days to refit the semi-gyros, after which we would demonstrate the viability of the navigation drill formulated for Vijayanta. I then took time to explain that a newly raised regiment would need some financial assistance for the modification and fitting of the semi-gyros on Vijayanta. This was promptly agreed upon and Colonel A. S. Rao was directed to issue a cheque from the Formations Annual Training Grant.

Meanwhile, Captain Manbir honoured his commitment—within 48 hours the semi-gyros arrived in the regiment. Light Repair Work shop (LRW) teams under Captain Jha, an efficient EME officer, got busy carrying out this local modification for fitting the cannibalized semi-gyros. The 4GB compass borrowed from the Air Force base at Kanpur had served us well when we had nothing in our hands except the standard compass prismatic issued by the ordnance. We were now the only Vijayanta regiment in the Armoured Corps, modifying the discarded semi-gyro of the PT-76 tank, using our own *jugaad*, indigenous skills and innovation to operationalize the semi-gyro fitted Vijayanta. Once put into operation, we got mixed responses and feedback from the crew on its practical utility during the exercise.

Regimental Briefing

My briefing was based on my personal experiences in life and war, insights from books and listening to the experiences of others. The long and short of what was conveyed was free of all jargon, the bare skin and bones of what response I expected from my subordinate commanders at all levels.

Young Officers

A young officer must cultivate the habit of 'casing the joint'—every time one moves into a new environment to quickly observe important features, layout of obstacles and mentally register the ground of tactical importance. This would help prepare you for a quick riposte. Flexibility and speed are crucial for tankmen.

Discipline

Discipline of an armoured unit differs from the rest of the army.

It is best illustrated by a pack of well-trained hounds, running in no set order. Success lies in the ability of each tank commander to understand his own position on the ground, the position of his troop leader and remain ever ready for action.

Judgement

The best man within the unit should not be the one who makes the least number of mistakes. Every new raising gets a fair percentage of NCOs and JCOs penalized by their officers for mistakes made in good faith. We must carefully watch out and tap the potential of such personnel, harness their talent and leadership skills for the good of the regiment.

Crew Members

Each member of the team must cultivate the qualities of initiative, alertness and the ability to quickly adapt to changing circumstances in order to be effective. The golden principle that applies is to keep moving and never sit still because one has no actual orders on what to do or how to do it.

Standing Operating Procedures

SOP and battle drills are good for training and serve as guidelines. In battle, no two situations will be similar. Compliance should be replaced with practical common sense; one must not follow the SOP slavishly.

Mental Preparedness

The hallmark of a genius is to be mentally alert and prepared, so that you can accept greater responsibility and execute it in the shortest possible time. This can take place at any level of command—with a troop if you are a JCO, or at the squadron level if you are an officer. Performing minor routine tasks efficiently prepares you to perform bigger tasks when the opportunity arises.

Intuition

Intuition or sixth sense arms an officer like no other. The tank commander who has absorbed military lessons during practical training finds readymade solution to respond to the developments on the battlefield due to his observation and intuition. It becomes a vital quality for a commander.

Audacity

Audacity must always be our battle cry. Be bold, be bold, always be bold. Act with boldness and vigour, tempered with good common sense. This is true in daily life as also on the battlefield.

Battle

As a commander you must absorb the tension while the tank crews execute your orders. Information about the enemy will never be complete. Risks have to be taken. The tank crew will follow your orders to escape the danger and thereby save their lives. This is what the heroic officer gives to the men in the hour of danger, lacking which, the whole unit is lost.

Second-in-command

The death of a commander can cause dislocation, crisis and even disaster. A well-trained unit must have the ability to 'carry on' even when the senior is wounded or killed. A responsible commander must ensure that his junior can take over from him with responsibility. Imagine the fate of the regiment if the commander becomes a casualty and the next senior officer fails to take charge due to professional incompetence.

Selection of Armoured Officers

Cavalry officers are expected to be quick to seize opportunities, be agile and remain cool-headed even under stress. Therefore only the very best are sent to the Armoured Corps. Elan, panache, chivalry, the spirit of adventure and ability to take risk is manifest in officers' early training and ethos. They must remember what they had learnt in the riding school: 'Make much of your horses'.

Exercise Brazen Chariots

14 Strike RAPID carried out Exercise Brazen Chariots IV as a precursor to the main exercise, but more particularly to test out the operational capability and preparation of the reorganized Mechanised Brigade of 14 Strike RAPID, in which 13 Armoured Regiment also participated. The exercise tested the integration of combat teams, combat groups and the functioning of the reorganized HQ Mechanised Brigade functioning under HQ Strike RAPID. The regiment tank crews were stunned at the end of the exercise when the Corps Commander Lieutenant General Hanut Singh came upon the regimental net to compliment the regiment for its operational readiness and the state of the desert conversion training. Considered a father figure of the Armoured Corps, his praise for all crews and outstations was heard loud and clear on the regimental radio net. It gladdened the hearts of all tank crews and continues to be recalled with pride to date. The morale of the regiment had skyrocketed. As the commandant, I realized that the general had not only infused us with a spirit that helps win battles but in so doing, had communicated the operational fitness of the regiment and the division as well.

Briefing by General Hanut Singh

The recce troop commander, an outstanding JCO, escorted me to HQ 2 Corps the next day. This was the first time in my service that I got to see a Strike Corps Tactical HQ deployed on the ground. I was ushered into the presence of Lieutenant General Hanut by his staff as if he was a revered soul. I had heard of him and had seen him from a distance but had never been briefed by him, or met him, except during the DAC conference at Delhi. Without any preamble, or other military courtesies, he spelt out his intent, stating that he would brief me on his concept of mobile warfare, which on return, I must share with my officers, as the regiment had joined his corps weeks after he had addressed all officers of the command regarding his concept of battle.

For the next 40 minutes, he dwelt on the important aspects of his larger philosophy and how it would integrate at the combat command, group and team levels. I sat there fully mesmerized by his soft voice, steely eyes and immaculate persona, his Adam's apple sticking out just above his blood-red scarf and fading grey jacket. He answered my queries at the end in precise, unambiguous terms. Just before departing, he delivered what came as a bolt from the blue: 'Another reason for calling you is because your GOC is weak. I expect you to hold his hand.' And the meeting ended.

On the way back, I reflected on why, like most other generals, he did not delegate this task to any subordinate or just send a letter conveying his thoughts. I realized that a letter could have communicated all the intellectual content of his thoughts. He chose to meet in person so that I could clear my doubts. As a sharp observer of human nature, he would watch a probable inflexion of the voice, or the expression of doubt, which could have revealed my response. The body language, gestures, words used and mannerisms, all add up to one's presence. The meeting was also a medium that conveyed his concept of battle and effectively imprinted his presence and visible passion. The ring in his voice and his solemn expression revealed his sincerity and personality. I learnt the power of personal briefing and how no letter can replace the aura of a face-to-face meeting with an outstanding soldier.

I can barely recall the 40 kilometre cross-country journey across sand dunes and then back to the regimental headquarters, as my head was spinning with the thoughts and ideas that I had picked up during the briefing along with the shocker delivered at the end. What stood out for me was his concept of battle—he understood that the battle groups are fluid, fast and nonlinear. Thus, the tendency to coordinate and control does not apply. By segmenting teams, both chaos and uncertainty increase but one gains in mobility what one loses in control. Mobility is the greatest force-multiplier. One had to disperse and concentrate to confuse and paralyze the enemy. I was to give my teams clear missions and then let them accomplish it as they deemed fit. The battle concept that I also learnt was that smaller teams were faster, more creative and more adaptable. It kept the officers and men more motivated. Fluidity brought more power and control.

If what I had experienced had not been shocking enough, a still bigger shock awaited me on my return. Two platoons of tank transporters were lined up just outside the regiment. A moustachioed colonel of the Army Supply Corps was observed brandishing his impressive notched cane at some driver. I stopped, only to be handed over a signal message received by him to ferry the regiment tanks to a new location. Those who had served with armoured formations in the past told me that this was a common practice. This was my first brush with armoured formations, having served with infantry divisions in the east. The regiment's tank drivers and commanders, through regular practice on mounting and dismounting Vijayanta on tank transporter vehicles, were confident and soon mounted. If anything, they were now doing it virtually blindfolded at night. The phrase 'train in peace to save blood in war' must have been coined in a similar situation by some ingenious soldier. The regiment was under move to its concentration area. Later in the night, the A1, A2, and B echelons were to move to the harbour before sunrise. The pace was beginning to match my temperament.

12

Conduct of Exercise Brasstacks

Phase I

Exercise Brasstacks had been announced and what followed was a spate of briefings at HQ 14 RAPID and Mechanised Brigade. I was pleasantly surprised to learn that two officers of 45 Cavalry, Major I. M. Singh and Major C. S. Ghosh, had been deputed as umpires on the regiment. The regiment was deployed in the open harbour during the day when the umpires arrived. As Brasstacks IV was scheduled to commence the same night, I thought it would be a good idea to bring all officers together into our field mess for a meal and have an informal chat with the umpires. The exercise was to run for seven nights, with a 24-hour non-tactical break before the commencement of Corps Phase II of the exercise. Amongst the many innovations, one important tactical grouping we had made was to place the technical officer, all recovery vehicles and LRW under the charge of the 2IC. Aware of the mechanical inefficiency of the Vijayanta engine, this group was well equipped to carry out urgent repair of tanks *in situ* by day and night. Tank crews were only to give location, after which it was the 2IC's job to ensure urgent repairs. In addition, the recce troop was split into sections so that a combination of recce sections and troop of tanks per squadron, fitted with semi-gyros, could work in unison to navigate the subunits through the unchartered desert terrain. Lastly, the logistics had been simplified. Each tank was to carry extra barrels, containing 200 litres of diesel, for replenishment. While the standard dry and emergency rations were distributed among troops, for crew cooking, I had taken the extra precaution of supplying each subunit with tinned rations. Further, I had arranged a special powder prepared by the Defence Food Laboratory in Mysore, which when mixed with flour, kept *chappatis* fresh for five days. This was based on a report I had read in the newspaper and had taken the initiative of sending a spunky SIC JCO to collect this novelty from the laboratory. This proved to be a big morale booster amongst troops who took great pleasure in sharing it and showing off amongst the combat teams in which they performed.

The two umpires were asked to mount the commandant tank to witness the grand spectacle of Exercise Brasstacks when unleashed at midnight across the international border. The tactical plan and location are not valid for those reading this nearly four decades after the conduct of Brasstacks IV. Up to four divisions had been launched across 150 kilometres of the exercise border, each leading with two combat groups. The independent armoured brigade and armoured division were on a different axis and were tasked for depth objectives of Corps Phase I. Two infantry divisions were to clear the axis and take over the isolation of the nodes that had been completed by Strike RAPID in Phase I. Strike RAPID was then to move forward to isolate and invest interim nodes and relieve armour for the Tank versus Tank Battle. The NMB (No Move Before) was fixed at midnight, when orders for advance were given by breaking radio silence.

It was a full moon night and visibility in the desert was very good. The leading combat team could be clearly seen ahead of my combat group HQs. I was accompanied by Lieutenant S. Jha, the IO and Captain Shashank Yadav, Regimental Signal Officer (RSO)—both of whom were livewires. The remaining two combat teams were towards the rear in double line formation, followed by the two logistic echelons further in the rear. Once the radio silence was lifted, the orders for starting engines were given. The smoke jettisoned from the exhaust of over 50 Armoured vehicles simultaneously grew into a large cloud. Along with that was the sound of powerful engines that suddenly broke the eerie silence of the night. On a given code the tanks switched on their parking lights and awaited the final order to advance. The whole operation was conducted like an orchestra, along with each individual tank commander reporting the completion of a specific task as per radio procedure. I could see the look of surprise and amazement on the faces of the two umpires. Like me, they too had never experienced such a spectacle as they had worked mostly with infantry formations. This display of raw power, coming alive with a single radio transmission across the 150-kilometre front was now being transformed into a mechanical giant that began its forward march to the music of engine horsepower, churning the trapped sand between the tracks through the sprockets. The entire corps cavalcade spread out within its tactical grouping, advancing rapidly through the night onto smaller tactical features, set along the course, to reach the first objective. The columns had raised thick clouds of smoke and dust through the night, well before the first light reports of isolation and enemy fire had filled the air. The sweat and the intense training carried out, and the high morale made Phase I of the division a complete success. By first light, we were well organized to take on the isolated enemy.

Phase II

By the end of Phase I, the regiment was asked to concentrate on a new exercise location. A 24-hour break virtually got telescoped into 12 hours, as the tanks had to extricate, be mounted on tank transporters, and we had to arrive at a new location. The regiment had a rough deal as troops were involved in an intensc activity from the day of arrival in the desert. The task of repair and recovery given to Randhir was especially gruesome as the Vijayanta would break down often due to engine failure. I gave brief instructions of what all had to be done within the available time frame before proceeding to the Division HQs for the briefing of Phase II of the corps/division plan. It was night by the time I arrived back at my RHQ. A radio message was sent earlier, asking for 'O' group to assemble at 2000 hours. While driving into the night harbour I realized that the tanks were lying unattended. On questioning this, I was informed that water trucks had arrived a short while ago and crews were out having a bath. It appeared a natural thing to do—the officers and tank crews hadn't bathed for nearly eight days. The task set out by the division were discussed and fresh orders were given out. It appeared from the reaction of the officers that everyone was tired, and their will to carry on was beginning to sag.

After the orders, Randhir requested to speak to me in private while the squadron commanders waited at some distance to hear the outcome of the meeting. He stated that the troops could no longer take strain from the intense activity of the last few days and demanded a longer break. He also implied that I was purposely flogging the regiment to win laurels for myself. He then added that he had discussed this with the other squadron commanders and their points of view were unanimous. While I was prepared to accept his individual plea, the fact that he was amassing supporters like that made me livid. I challenged him to put that down in writing and that I would take the disobedience of orders in field service to its logical end. I also explained how the 24-hour halt had got telescoped due to orders emanating from the corps and division level. His initial defiance was beginning to gradually wane when the overall circumstances were explained. He had misread the larger picture, partly due to his own individual disposition and from being influenced by the collective response of the squadron commanders. His initial bravado was beginning to mellow down, and he appeared pacified by my brief explanation. I sensed that his Rajput pride and assurance to other squadron commanders to get orders reversed were now disturbing him. Also, admitting an error of judgement, which amounted to a loss of face, was hurting him. It was at this juncture, that a wise and seasoned soldier, the Quartermaster Sayal, who must have been standing outside the shelter, walked in and forcefully dragged Randhir away. Sayal returned a short while later to say that Randhir had been drinking and had got carried away and would now like to apologize. The squadron commanders had, by now, returned to their squadrons. Word was sent out that all night maintenance of tanks would continue without a break and harbour struck the next morning before first light.

Randhir was a strong man, neither obstinate, nor pig-headed. After the showdown, he returned in a few minutes, looking more sober, to apologize with dignity. He grew in my esteem, as he had the courage and character to share his anxiety and concern face to face with me. He never brought up this incident again. It reflected his blue blood and pride in his Rajput upbringing and confirmed my belief that his loyalty could never be doubted.

Regardless of the political developments and the media reportage of the time, I was determined to ensure my regiment played its part unflinchingly. With gruff solicitude, I made up my mind to teach the officers what discipline was demanded during a war-like situation. It was difficult for subordinate officers to understand the pressure and tension of command as well as the fact that one had to suffer it in silence. Quite like the others, I too was exhausted and needed my forty winks. I called for Jha and Yadav and told them I had ordered an all-night maintenance parade. As members of my tank crew, their conduct would automatically transmit a message to the squadrons. The A2 and B echelon crews were whistled up to assist in the maintenance of the tanks. A surprise inspection by the commandant had already been announced. Having rested for some time, I started going around the squadrons at 0100 hours. While many crew members were working, most squadron commanders had to be jolted out of the comfort of their B echelon bedding and put back on supervising the maintenance of their squadrons. None resisted, most were thankful. Few would forget the cold desert night for some years to come. If I sounded the alarm for them, they dutifully passed it through their command, forming a chain reaction. All this must have added up in some measure of goodness for the regiment, for the Corps Phase II went off without a hitch due to the excellent work done by the squadrons.

I recall interacting with one of the squadron officers one night:

> Me: 'Have the men had a hot meal and bath?'
>
> Officer: 'Yes, Sir. The meal was delayed as the water trucks got held up.'
>
> Me: 'Was the spare time used for the maintenance of the tanks?'
>
> Officer: 'No, Sir, the men were tired. So, I gave them a break.'
>
> Me: 'We are out on an exercise, not a picnic, Surely it's a task which has to be completed for Phase II.'
>
> Officer: 'Yes, Sir.'
>
> Me: 'Were you able to interact with the crews after the meal?'
>
> Officer: 'Yes, Sir. I joined them for the meal.'
>
> Me: 'What is their feedback? Are they liking it?'
>
> Officer: 'Yes, Sir. May I speak frankly?'
>
> Me: 'Of course! Why not?'
>
> Officer: 'Sir, I can sum up their feeling in one sentence.'
>
> Me : 'Yes, let me hear it.'

Officer: 'Sir, fucked and far from home—especially the drivers.'
Me: 'And you?'
Officer: 'Sir, we have Phase II coming.'
Me: 'So, how do you feel? Too tired? Exhausted?'
Officer: 'No, Sir. I am fine.'
Me: 'I think your men have rested enough. It is past 0100 hours. Get cracking with maintenance. I will be back soon.'

I was in the SHQ of another squadron a little later. The squadron commander and all tank crews were fast asleep. One crew member of the guard tank responded to my presence.

Sentry: '*Jai Hind, Saab ji.*' (Long Live India, Saheb!)
Me: 'Squadron commander *ka tank kidhar hai*?' (Where is the squadron commander's tank?)
En route I asked, '*Khana kitne baje khaya?*' (When did you eat?)
Sentry: '*8 baje, Saab.*' (At 8, Sir.)
Me: '*Kya mila khane mein?*' (What were you served?)
Sentry: '*Dal, roti, chawal, aur chicken curry, Saab.*' (Dal, chapati, rice and chicken curry, Sir.)
Me: '*Shabash.*' (Good!)

By now we were close to the Squadron HQ. There was the silence of a graveyard, except for the sound of some snoring. The officer accompanying me, Yadav, moved forward to wake the squadron commander up.

Yadav: 'Sir, the CO is here.'
Officer: 'Hello, Sir, just getting ready, Sir.'
Me: 'Don't bother.'

I paused long enough for him to gather his wits. What I was

horrified to see was this officer stepping out in a colourful sleeping suit from under an equally colourful thick quilt. I waited long enough for him to adjust his headgear. Randhir stood alongside.

Me: 'Randhir, what orders were given about maintenance?'
Randhir: 'Night-long maintenance of the tanks, Sir.'
Me: 'Additional crews of A1 and A2 echelons were sent to the squadrons to help the tank crews?'
Randhir: 'Yes, Sir.'
Me: 'Instead of putting them to work, you and your men are sleeping?'

One of the officers joined our conversation

Officer: 'The men are very tired after seven days of movement, Sir.'
Me: 'We are all tired, but the Corps Phase II is not going to stop because men are tired.'
Officer: 'Sir, I have been part of a lot of exercises with my regiment in Ambala, but it has never been like this.'
Me: 'I know about your previous regiment—stuck in Ambala for 12 years. Your exercises were conducted in areas adjoining the unit area. Do not quote your previous regiment. Why are you flouting direct orders from me?'
Officer: 'I had given them time to rest till first light and do maintenance after that.'
Me: 'At first light I plan to move the regiment. Get your men up now, up their dead asses and on their dying feet.'
Officer: 'Yes, Sir.'
Me: 'No bloody "Yes, Sir." Give the order now and mount your tanks, while I light up.'
Randhir: 'Sir, you have given him a mouthful.'
Me: 'Bloody shit! Pink pyjamas in the battle zone. And where the

hell did he get a quilt from? Fucking soldiering!'

Randhir: 'Yes, Sir, it is either two blankets or an overcoat and a blanket like you, Sir.'

Me: 'Let's move on.'

It took another ten minutes before we reached the next squadron. Word must have gone around that the 'tiger' was on the prowl. The senior officer was fortunately in his dungarees and not pink pyjamas. He greeted me more cheerfully to say that the boys were now well-rested and maintenance tasks were underway. He assured me that his tank crews were raring to go and would take on any task assigned. Though tired, he appreciated that we had to do much more to win a good name as a new regiment. The brigade commander had travelled on his tank during Phase I and was all praise for the battle drills and positive response of our troop leaders. A cup of tea appeared out of nowhere with a young NCO, cheerful after his short nap, saying, '*Sirji, chak de phatte!*'[2] It was time to get back and have a quick look at the map and ready myself for the incoming radio call from General Pillai.

Phase II of Exercise Brasstacks commenced with the break of dawn. While maintenance was in progress, the cookhouses and logistics were working overtime. A hot breakfast and packed lunches were delivered to all, along with fresh packets of *shakarparas* and an additional roll of chapati carrying the preservative obtained from Mysore. This small initiative, taken while reading a newspaper report on this preservative at Kanpur, became a great public relation exercise amongst the troops the unit worked with. On the tactical side, the combat teams worked in close cooperation with the infantry brigades and were able to win their confidence and admiration for their professional conduct and willingness to help. Major

[2] A phrase of encouragement in Punjabi

General K. C. Tewari, GOC 4 Infantry Division, was a senior umpire during Exercise Brasstacks and was keeping a close watch on the performance of the unit. Flying overhead in a helicopter, watching a manoeuvre conducted by the regiment, he landed near my tank to compliment the regiment for its sterling performance. As a senior umpire he was privy to daily briefings from all the umpires including enemy exercise. This was a rare compliment for the regiment.

An air of jubilation rented the air when the code word to end Exercise Brasstacks was issued on the radio. Units were allotted areas where they were to go into open harbour. The logistic tail consisting of vehicles of the A1, A2 and B echelons soon linked up with the F echelons in the harbour. Tents were set up and arrangements for piping hot food and water points were established overnight. The tank troops had roughed it out for nearly a fortnight without the basic creature comforts that were now being laid out. The fundamental principle of 'make much of your horses', and old cavalry tradition still had to be adhered to by tank crews. This implied topping up of tanks, essential maintenance and repair. A lot of warm hand shakes, back slapping and *shabash* would be exchanged followed by catching up with letters from friends and relatives. The tinkle of glasses and piping hot food would be imbibed while they would exchange their experiences before retiring to spend a night of relative comfort in the meagre bedding and personal effects brought up by the B echelon.

While the formation commanders were to attend the summing up of Exercise Brasstacks at the Tactical Headquarters of 2 Corps, a message was received that all formations and the units would hold campfires and *barakhanas*. Transport restrictions had been lifted to facilitate movement of troops to attend these functions. This was soon followed by invitations from units of Strike RAPIDs, specially the adhoc Mechanised Brigade. An informal meeting of squadron commanders and senior JCO, was held to ascertain their views on holding our unit camp fire. Having heard the views of everyone, I announced that instead of a unit camp fire now, we would celebrate on returning to Kanpur when the families could also join in. As a large number of armoured regiments had participated in this exercise and were in close proximity of the location, why not permit each individual the choice to attend the campfire with his previous parent unit. Those whose previous units were not present in Brasstacks could be detailed to attend campfires with local units from which invitations had been received. This simple decision took many by surprise, as a large number were yearning to revisit their old regiments, especially the JCO and jawans. This was a golden chance for them to go back to their previous units and attend the campfires with old friends and comrades. I went one step beyond by making it compulsory for everyone. Transport details were coordinated and 48 hours were given to these groups to return back to the camp. This decision helped the unit immensely, as each one had an opportunity of listening from others about their performance, instead of their own officers and the CO drumming paeans upon them. This gave the unit personnel the confidence, a sense of pride and the realization that while old regiments had a sense of pride and achievement almost married to them, a new raising too can match them by dint of performance and sincere effort, sometimes even outperforming them.

The last two to leave were the umpires from 45 Cavalry, my previous regiment. They did their best to convince me to accept the invitation to celebrate with them. However, I declined and said, 'One has my heart, the other my name', confident that I bore no anger or ill will. They departed soon after.

The overall feedback received by the time Exercise Brasstacks ended was that our Vijayanta had outperformed more than a dozen Vijayanta regiments deployed for the exercise. It was ahead of some of the recently inducted T-72 regiments in terms of mileage during the exercise. A comparison carried out at the Command HQs revealed that the tanks of 13 AR had clocked over 600 kilometres and had an on-road state of 92 per cent, thanks to the dedicated recovery team under the 2IC. The news of how this newly raised regiment converted the 4GB compass into semi-gyros, floated across the mechanised forces. A special mention of 13 AR at the corps summing up, followed by praise showered by General Hanut and General Pillai on the achievements and level of operational efficiency and cooperation with other arms, swept everyone off their feet.

Success has many masters. In this case, it was doubly true. Now it was time to bask in the glory of a job well done. A new sense of pride enveloped the regiment. This became more manifest after the campfire, when the tank crews visited their previous units to attend *barakhanas*. The exchange of *langar gup* is a very strong way to gauge performance and reputation and improve self-esteem. Many JCOs and NCOs returned with intense pride on hearing from their ex-comrades about how well 13 AR had performed during Exercise Brasstacks. The sincere hard work, sense of honour, devotion to their officers and the spirit and readiness to go anywhere and do anything displayed by the officers, as well as the rank and file of the regiment over the course of 10 weeks became the moral foundation and spirit of this regiment. The GOC further claimed recognition for being the only formation to have equipped tanks of 13 AR with semi-gyros procured from CAFVD, Kirkee. In addition to this, the troops tasked for operations with this regiment were full of praise for the logistics and food shared by the tank crews, as they carried chapatis baked with preservatives supplied by the defence laboratory in Mysore, which remained fresh through the exercise. More importantly, the spirit of cooperation and cohesion at all levels was applauded by everyone. To hear all this from ex-comrades and officers from one's former regiment replaced the pain of separation, instilling a new sense of belief and respect for the oft-repeated magic of *Tehra Sab Tera.*

While still deployed in the desert, waiting for the military special train to take us back to Kanpur, a message was received from the

Corps HQ asking the units to submit lessons learnt during Exercise Brasstacks. This is part of the standard practice. The feedback received from units is tabulated and after due discussions and deliberation at interim HQs finally included in the training directive. Though units spend long hours finalizing this document, inputs projected by units are mostly of more practical nature and rarely receive due weightage, Shashank and Jha, functioning as my radio and intelligence officers, were mustered to give finishing touches to a caricature drawn on the reverse of a file cover during a brief interlude during the exercise. Jha was good at sketching, and together we were able to etch out a rough impression of a tank commanders view of Exercise Brasstacks and gave it the caption LAW-87 (Land and Air War 1987).This was later despatched with a covering letter under my signature as Lessons Learnt to the Corps HQ. As nothing was heard for the next few days, I took it that our amateurish attempt had been consigned to the waste basket by some humourless staff officer.

The bulk of the regiment personnel and wheeled vehicles moved by road in convoy under the charge of Major Virender. The tanks remained in harbour and would be transported back by rail over the next two weeks. I took a few days off to join my wife and children for a short vacation. We were able to traverse the entire desert belt, with halts at Jaisalmer, Udaipur, Jodhpur and Bharatpur, before returning to Kanpur.

13

Debrief and Demit

A few weeks after my return to Kanpur, we received a signal from HQ 2 Corps, directing me to attend the debrief at HQ 14 Strike RAPID at Dehradun. I was looking forward to this debrief as it would give me an opportunity to meet all the brigade commanders and other commanding officers who had sent letters of appreciation to the regiment and, of course, General Pillai and his staff officers. It turned out to be a large gathering, with some of the umpire and corps staff also present. These debriefs are formal sessions in which commanders highlight the lessons learnt and make recommendations, if any. The entire event is structured and follows a laid-down format. Many of the commanders and GOC Pillai commented on the satisfactory performance of 13 AR. This was exceptional as any direct reference to specific units is not the norm and thus usually avoided. When it was time for the corps commander to address all the officers, he spoke on the initial planning, the disruption caused due to Pakistan's movement of their Army reserves followed by our reaction announcing Operation Trident in response to Pakistan's Operation Sledgehammer, thus leading to a war-like situation between the two countries. Operation Trident necessitated troops being sucked away for operational deployment, especially the Mechanised Brigades of Strike RAPID. The decision to conduct Exercise Brasstacks led to a few changes and the creation of the ad hoc Mechanised Brigade. He complimented the officers on their dedication and exemplary conduct. He then thanked all commanders for the written feedback they had shared, which would be analysed and then circulated as lessons learnt. He then placed his hands on the lectern and pulled out the file cover, which carried the caricature we had sent as our feedback. General Hanut took great pleasure in displaying it to the assembled officers of Strike RAPID and the umpires. He held it out for all to see, briefly describing his own appreciation of a remarkable feedback. The corps commander read out the caption: 'Land and Air Warfare-87 (LAW-87)' and expressed his happiness at the performance of the regiment. He asked me to come forward and collect it, suggesting that this be displayed in the bar of officers' mess. While handing over the file cover, he broke protocol and asked me to briefly explain LAW-87.

I spoke of how the feedback was a collective effort of my tank crew—the sketch showed Corps Commander General Hanut mounted on a horseback, overseeing his formations, represented by the branches of the tree, moving across the desert along their thrust lines, advancing towards their objectives. The divisional commanders were depicted performing a Red Indian style war dance around the tree, celebrating the successful operations. General Hanut was the high priest of mobile warfare and was, thus, 'in the saddle', watching his commanders while keeping an eye on the sacrificial goat, 13 AR, tied to the tree trunk. The presence of guns, airplanes, nodes and sand dunes is a depiction of the LAW-87. I justified the depiction of 13 AR as the sacrificial goat as it had barely completed raising five months before the start of Exercise Brasstacks. The regiment had been raised on War Establishment for plains but had been deployed in the desert from three different stations, while participating in the Republic Day parade to form part of a Mechanised Brigade of a Strike RAPID. The unit had to reorganize and train for participation while carrying out modifications to the equipment and training the Armoured Fighting Vehicle (AFV) crews and tradesmen. This sketch reflected the thinking of the unit and its personnel. I then added that the Vijayanta tank had numerous drawbacks, but from day one of the raising, we had christened it as the best-known tank of the Third World. Prior to the commencement of the exercise, we had centralized all repair and recovery under the 2IC Major Randhir, who made sure that our off-road state[1] was minimal.

I then surprised everyone by telling them that my association with 2 Corps went back to the 1971 war. My regiment, 45 Cavalry, was part of 2 Corps when my squadron destroyed the 3 (Independent) Armoured Squadron of Pakistan in the Tank versus Tank Battle on 21 November 1971. Thirteen years later, I was to raise 13 Armoured Regiment and felt privileged to have participated with the same 2 Corps, under the leadership of the 'high priest'. The only lesson that I would be taking back with me was *Tehra Sab Tera.*

On returning to the Kanpur squadron, *barakhanas* were organized and families in station were also invited. A special *sainik sammelan* was organized to celebrate the resilience and regimental team spirit. A strong foundation had been laid due to the collective grit and might of all squadrons. Our coming together was once again a beautiful reminder that teamwork is a daily habit, it is what makes the regimental flag. Each, by his own capacity but equal in his dedication and sincerity, makes the flag, which in turn determines who we are within the galaxy of the larger Armoured Corps.

It was now time to do something for the officers' mess, which I

[1] Vehicles which need repairs before they can be utilized on duty or deployed for military duties

had kept as the last regimental institution on my original priority list. The logic was simple—a translation of the old cavalry code 'Make much of your horses'. This was tacitly combined with the cardinal principle etched in Chetwode Hall at IMA, the cornerstone of military leadership for officers: 'Your own welfare, last always and every time'. A mess meeting was held, and the ladies were invited as special guests. We set priorities within the available budget and set up a purchase committee to get the bare essentials for a functional officers' mess. Trips were organized for officers' families and ORs to visit the month-long annual mela at Gwalior, where household items were sold at subsidized prices. After basic purchases were made, officers and their families visited the carpet factory at Bareilly. While the officers made purchases as per their requirements, they all got together to buy the first carpet for the officers' mess. The one that was unanimously agreed upon turned out to be an export extra, in the size 13'x13', which covered the exact area of the main lounge of an old residential building that had been allotted to the regiment as the officers' mess on the banks of river Ganga.

Life in the unit is so busy and strenuous that even while the celebrations post Brasstacks were taking place, a spate of fresh commitments and directives started arriving from HQ 4 Infantry Division—training, conferences, visits, games and competitions. Word was received that the Army commander Central Command would be visiting the regiment. Soon after this visit, Randhir walked up with a faint smile to share that he had been sounded by his regimental officer, working in the Military Secretary branch, handling postings and promotions of officers, that he had been cleared for promotion and command of 13 Armoured Regiment. His reluctance to step into the command saddle was still manifest, even while he openly expressed gratitude for my recommendation. I assured him that he richly deserved the promotion, and it was hugely satisfying to hand over command to a deserving officer, who would carry forward the work we had undertaken together over the last two-and-a-half years. The news spread quickly, followed by the arrival of a formal signal, announcing my posting and Randhir's appointment.

A few days later, as the formalities of handover were completed, I sat down to write my last special order of the day and bid farewell.

Colonel B. S. Mehta
13 Armoured Regiment
C/0 56 APO
1509/6/A
7 June 1987

1. *This regiment was raised by the collective effort of all officers, JCOs and ORs on the rolls of the regiment during the period 21 December 1984 – 4 June 1987.*
2. *Raising a regiment is like riding bareback. The struggle is harder; the sweat, toil and tears unending. The reward is confidence in our own abilities, understanding and respect for the esprit de corps of the cavalry, and regimental pride.*
   We are proud of our unique identity—13 Armoured Regiment, our badge, flag, colours, demonstrated performance in all fields of regimental activity—the foundations of the 13 family.
3. *Pride is the sum total of many tangibles and intangibles of the regimental system. Success and recognition are important ingredients. We worked for it.*
4. *13 Armoured Regiment has grown as the child prodigy of the Armoured Corps. The high priest and many others have said so. The expectations and quality of excellence demanded of us will be much higher. The regimental ethos is that we never give up. This has, and will, hold us in good stead to ensure rapid growth.*
5. *Change of command is a stage of growth. I am happy to hand over*

to Lieutenant Colonel Randhir Singh. Give him and the regiment your best.

6. *The Special Order—and the last one. Join hands to build on the foundation. Strive harder so that the Armoured Corps remains proud of you.*

Good Luck. God Bless and Goodbye.
Veer Bhogya Vasundhara

A re-creation of LAW-87, the sketch sent as feedback to General Hanut Singh after Exercise Brasstacks. This re-creation was made by Colonel Bhupinder Singh (14H/45C).

Appendices

Letter from General Hanut Singh

ले० जनरल हनूत सिंह, एम वी सी
जनरल आफसर कमांडिंग
Lt Gen Hanut Singh MVC
General Officer Commanding

मुख्यालय २ कोर
द्वारा ५६ ए पी ओ
Headquarters 2 Corps
C/o 56 APO

6126/HS/1

29 Apr 87

My dear Bikram,

1. Thank you for your letter dated 29 Mar 87 and for the interesting feed back that you have given on Exercise Brass Tacks IV.

2. Initially, 16 Armd Bde and 23 Armd Bde were earmarked to constitute the Mech Bdes of 14 & 36 Strike RAPIDs and they were trained for this role. Subsequently, because of Op TRIDENT, both these Bdes could not participate and 13 Armd Regt and 76 Armd Regt were inducted in their place in order to form adhoc mech bdes of the two Strike RAPIDs. I was naturally apprehensive because your Regiment was not only a new raising, but was also new to the entire concept of functioning as a part of a Strike RAPID, which in itself is a totally new concept, and it had no previous experience of operating in desert terrain. However, a regt is a reflection of its CO and I was reassured when I learnt that you were commanding 13 Armd Regt. I was confident that with your experience, incl battle experience, and with your dedication to the profession, you would have brought 13 Armd Regt to a good standard of trg already, notwithstanding the short period since its raising. I was further confident that once you were apprised of what would be required of you, you would be able to quickly make up whatever shortfalls there were in your training and would be able to take your place as a part of the Mech Bde of 14 RAPID.

3. The performance of 13 Armd Regt, both in Ex Brazen Charriots IV and in Ex Brass Tacks IV, has justified the confidence I reposed in your ability as a CO, and in your Regt. You were not only able to carry out the tasks assigned to you but were also able to do so in a commendable manner.

...2/

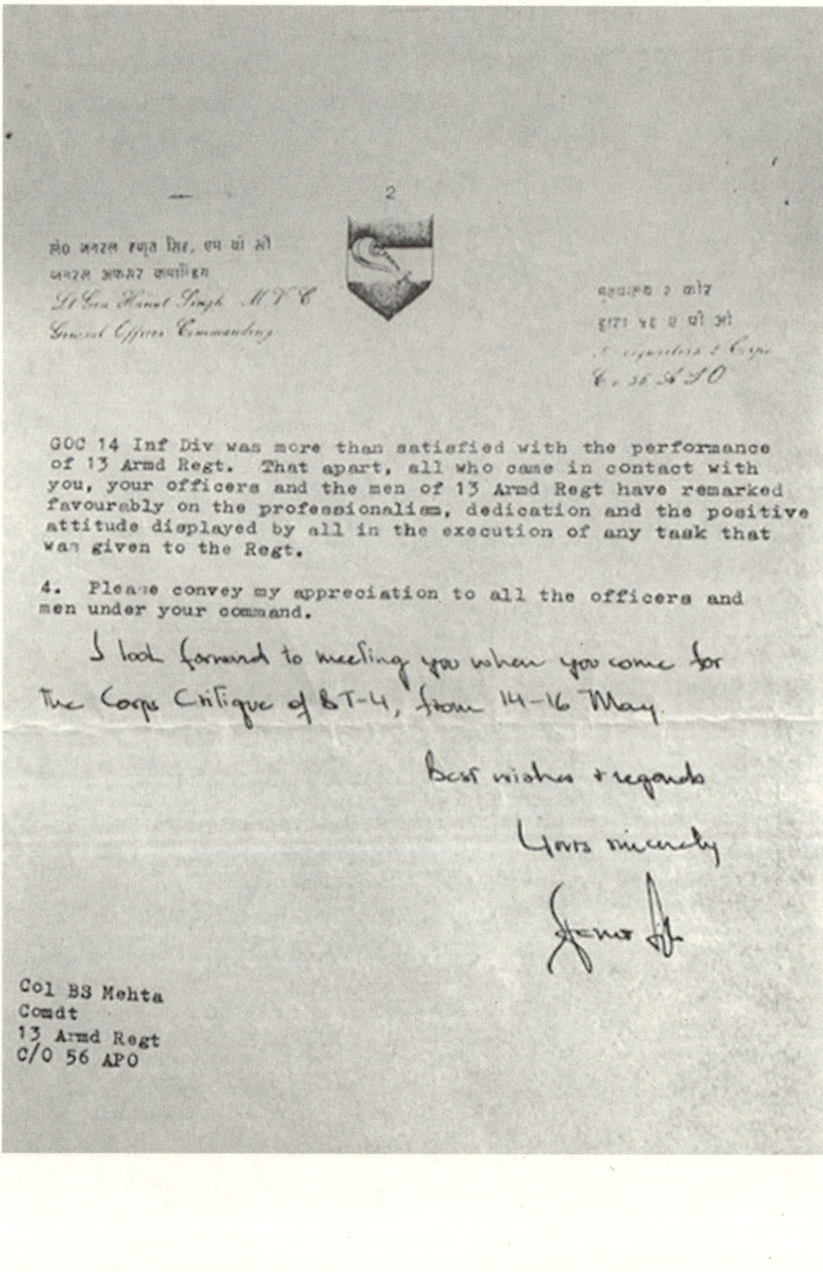

2

Lt Gen Hanut Singh MVC
General Officer Commanding

Headquarters 2 Corps
C/o 56 APO

GOC 14 Inf Div was more than satisfied with the performance of 13 Armd Regt. That apart, all who came in contact with you, your officers and the men of 13 Armd Regt have remarked favourably on the professionalism, dedication and the positive attitude displayed by all in the execution of any task that was given to the Regt.

4. Please convey my appreciation to all the officers and men under your command.

I look forward to meeting you when you come for the Corps Critique of BT-4, from 14-16 May.

Best wishes + regards

Yours sincerely

Hanut Singh

Col BS Mehta
Comdt
13 Armd Regt
C/O 56 APO

Letter from Major General S. K. Pillai

मेजर जनरल एस. के. पिल्ले
जनरल अफसर कमान
Maj Gen S K Pillai
General Officer Commanding

मुख्यालय
Headquarters
१४ इन्फेंट्री डिवीजन
14 Infantry Division
द्वारा ५६ एपीओ
C/o 56 APO

7325/SKP/1

27 Mar 87

My Dear Balram,

1. This is to express my sense of deep appreciation for the work done by your Regiment during Brass Tacks. Your Regiment has also earned the appreciation of the Inf Bdes with whom your Sqns functioned. The Bde Cdrs have remarked on the willingness and energetic spirit of your offrs and men in carrying out the joint tasks. This speaks highly of the standard of leadership and professional competence of a Regiment, which even though newly raised, has acquitted itself very well.

2. Please express my appreciation to your offrs and men on behalf of 14 Inf Div. I am sending a small memento to commemorate our association.

With best wishes

Yours sincerely

Sushil

Col Balram Mehta
Commanding Officer
13 Armd Regt
C/O 56 APO

Journey from a Pip to Param Vishisht[1]

Often people who criticize your life are the same people that don't know the price you paid to get where you are today.

-Shannon Akler

On 8 January 1985, a young pipper set foot in the Mecca of Armoured Corps at Ahmednagar. All excited, albeit with lot of circumspection, to embark on an unknown mission, as part of a hitherto unknown outfit (we didn't have shoulder numerals or badge). The 'lost' look attracted the attention of a burly Sikh JCO, who walked up querying quizzically, 'Jha Sahab?' It came as a big relief, since the railway station had emptied out by then. Introducing himself as Risaldar Jagjit Singh from 13 Armoured Regiment, he quickly packed me with my NDA box and IMA Officers' Issue Kit and bedroll on a Shaktiman, lent by the Driving and Maintenance Regiment (DMR) to the newly raised unit, 13 Armoured Regiment.

From then onwards till I hung up spurs at Ahmednagar on 31 October 2021, life as a cavalier was a rollercoaster ride, full of trials and tribulation, satisfaction and frustration, joy and sorrow, and so on. Indeed, a package deal of life worthy of being relived, only if permitted again.

Being a second-generation army brat, the Armed Forces were not new, but Armoured Corps was indeed an enigma. And the mystery further deepened when one met the Commandant Colonel Balram Singh Mehta (later Brigadier) and the 2IC Major Randhir Singh (God bless his soul).

And so, the journey started as a Dashing Troop Leader (DTL) at Ahmednagar, and Kanpur followed gradually, filling all

[1] This piece was penned by the first directly commissioned officer of the regiment, then Second Lieutenant Shailjanand Jha, who retired as Major General. He was awarded the Param Vishisht Seva Medal.

appointments tenable at the regimental level.

In this journey spanning over 36 years, the most interesting phase of the first 20 years, which was also the most educative one, started with 13 Armoured Regiment. This voyage laid the foundation and shaped the profile of my career. It was characterized by ambiguity and mystery.

Having taken birth in a unit which itself was yet to take birth and stand on its feet as a fighting outfit, it necessitated innovating and adapting not only to establish oneself as the leader with his superiors and peers but also to integrate the men one had to lead into a team. Not to forget that one had to master the equipment, the Vijayanta, that too in an environment where one was learning about the 'animal', while others including the men, already adept at handling the animal, were only converting to a different name. The degree of difficulty can be visualized from the fact that all this was to be achieved with no administrative, logistic, monetary, or training infrastructure intrinsic to an established outfit. It required foresight and individual as well as organizational grit of a different kind. They say that a regiment remains a new raising till its first original officer commands the regiment and the first original soldier becomes its Risaldar Major.

Kudos to the first eight commandants, especially the founder, Colonel Balram Mehta (retired as Brigadier), who set the ball rolling at a pace and direction that despite being a fixed class regiment facing multiple tests and tribulations including Exercise Brasstacks, and thereafter despite being undone into a mixed class regiment, the regiment continued to stand up to its Greek equivalent name Triskaideca with pride and glory. The six commandants to follow Lieutenant Colonel Randhir Singh, who came from other established setups further added the value, muscle, heft and ethos to make Triskaideca one of the finest fighting outfits within the Armoured Corps.

I took over the regiment as its ninth commandant, which not only saw 13 shed its 'new raising' prefix but also entailed de-facto conversion from a unit deployed for defensive operational tasks to a unit tailored for offensive tasks and equipped with state-of-the-art T-90 tanks, which it holds as of date. This phase of a regimental voyage put one, once again, into the grind of raising, but with a difference. The challenge was to change the mindset of an organizationally integrated unit and set the stage for excellence in manoeuvre warfare, equipped with an entirely new generation of equipment. The resistance of subunit level autonomy with just armour ingredient, which the officers and men were used to, had to be replaced with the philosophy of 'disaggregated initiation, oriented towards aggregated application at the point of decision' in a combined arms structure. The approach adopted was to re-raise it bottom upwards, unlike the first raising, which was top-down. The NCOs and JCOs, who were the permanent entities and well-versed with the new equipment, had to be empowered, since by now the regiment had to operate with critical hard scales, unlike earlier when there was no shortage of officers. This was a grinding process, which finally ended when I demitted regimental command in December 2006. The journey since command was an exciting and exhilarating experience, one that ended as Commandant, Armoured Corps Centre and School in 2021. I had the privilege of becoming Colonel of Triskaideca once again, in the last five years of my career—a privilege very few get, and one that gave me immense pride, since the regiment had, in its 36 years, not only proved its mettle in many difficult assignments but also enriched itself with glories including Unit Citation for outstanding performance.

Norman Dixon in his seminal work *On the Psychology of Military Incompetence* states that every man in uniform reaches his limit of incompetence. I had reached mine. As I hung up spurs after a final ride on 'Tauqat', the glamorous stallion in Nagar, I said to myself,

Well Shail, you 'pip', you have become a 'Param Vishisht' in an exciting journey. You contributed to the best of your capability and your perseverance has been recognized not just by the regiment, Corps and Army but the nation as well. Time to 'fade away' from the Armed Forces and embark on yet another challenge, another enigma.

A big salute to all my superiors who groomed me, peers who cheered me and subordinates who instilled and inspired the values in me, which ultimately armed me with the weapons to pursue the life of a professionally honest soldier. Triskaideca, you made it happen. *Tehra Sab Tera.*

Major General Shailjanand Jha
PVSM, VSM (Retired)
Dec. 1984 – Oct. 2021
13 Armoured Regiment C/0 56 APO

Reminiscences

Colonel Vinod Kochhar recalls his experience after joining 13 AR in January 1985:

> On my reporting to the regiment in January 1985, I was asked by the founder commandant during my interview as to which squadron I would like to raise. Since I was the OC of the 'C' squadron in my old regiment I quickly announced that I would like to raise the 'C' squadron, knowing little that I was going to land up with the Rajputs of Rajasthan, Haryana, UP and MP. The first battle was named the Battle of Sahayaks. No *sahayak* would come to me, and my squadron officers kept complaining to me; I in turn kept requesting the senior JCO Risaldar Shambhoo Singh, who was not only huge by built but had long moustaches as a Rajput warrior. Every time he would push his moustache upwards and announce, 'Sir, *kal aa jayega*' (He will come tomorrow, Sir.). That '*kal*' never came till I cornered him and asked about the problem. The problem was that Rajput honour was such that nobody wanted to polish the shoes. I had to take special permission to hold a *sainik sammelan,* and I asked the senior JCO to make the boys who refused to be *sahayaks* sit in the front row without making it obvious. I carried a boot brush, polish tin and a piece of cloth in a paper bag. After covering all the relevant points, I touched upon administration and asked the front row to stand up and remove the shoes. I said I would polish the shoes of the boys and see if I became a cobbler from the squadron commander. The boys refused to remove the shoes. Till the time I remained in the regiment, and even after, nobody ever refused to be my *sahayak.* To date I am in touch with two *sahayaks,* and I have been to their villages in Bihar and Kerala for their marriages, accompanied by my wife.

An extract from the diary of Major M. A. Shah elucidates the transition from the Republic Day parade to a sudden induction into the desert.

> Neighbourly relations had worsened around that time with our unfriendly neighbour Pakistan, so immediately after the Republic Day parade in 1987, we (tanks, men and all vehicles) were bundled off to the Railway Station in the Delhi Cantonment and put on a special train to Suratgarh, where we reached by the month-end and joined the rest of 13 Armoured Regiment, who had been camping on the sand *tibbas* near the Suratgarh Railway Station.
>
> I do not remember too many details of the next two months spent in the desert of Rajasthan. Suffice it to say that they were the most gruelling and tiring months of my life... Balram was a hard taskmaster and he had us by the short hairs! We would move and set up camp from one location to another, but we were always under the watchful eye of the Regimental Headquarters. The desert sands took their toll on the mechanical efficiency of the Vijayantas, so quite some time was spent on their repair and recovery, and, of course, I made good use of the opportunity of being in the desert by shooting quite a few partridges (despite contrary orders on the subject)! We did a lot of night navigation on the tanks. In those days, since there was no GPS on the tanks, we had to rely on the obsolete prismatic compass, night stars and a good sense of direction. Balram got hold of some aircraft compass and told me to go and check its efficacy in the desert by placing it on top of the tank turret—it was worthless, and I cursed and cursed as I sat on top of a tank in the cold desert night gallivanting away! That night I almost decided to put in my papers and leave the Army, but thank God I did not. During that time, I once again became close to my Khalsa troops—they were always cheerful, never complaining, and a hot, steaming mug of tea was always ready for me at the drop of a hat. The main exercise, Brasstacks, lasted for 14 days and nights.

> We used to catch a bit of shut eye whenever there was a lull in the battle, but my tank headphones never came off. Yes, once again, better sense prevailed upon both India and Pakistan and the jolly old balloon came floating down instead of going up. We were back in our stables at Kanpur by around early April 1987.

Another extract from Major M. A. Shah's memoir:

> Holi in March/April 1985. I distinctly remember this occasion because I feel that it was the first event that brought about a little bonding between the troops from various regiments to become part of 13 Armoured Regiment. For the Rajput boys it was a big festive occasion, for the South Indians it was just another holiday, but it was the Sikhs who were still smarting after Operation Blue Star, absolutely cold and unenthusiastic. It became quite obvious when they refused to have any *gulal* put on themselves, just about tasted the sweetmeats offered to them and sat glumly in a congregation, waiting for the parade to get over. But their gloomy mood was short-lived. Once all officers, JCOs and men sat down in a huddle on a couple of tarpaulins spread on the ground and a dholki appeared out of nowhere with the furniture NCO Om Singh on the mike as an impromptu master of ceremonies, and pakoras, rum and soft drinks did the rounds, their mood also melted, and they became part and parcel of the happy crowd. '*Na mera hai, na uska hai, bas tehra hi tera hai*'[1] got the loudest cheering and applause. Somebody sang a song, and everyone joined in. Then somebody sang a *ragini,* and soon we switched to non-vegetarian stuff as there were no ladies around! By the time we all dispersed, we were a happier lot. And yes, the Khalsas were just as bathed in colour as the rest, instead of being spotlessly clean as they were in the beginning of the proceedings!

[1] A celebratory song dedicated to 13 AR

List of Abbreviations and Acronyms

13 AR: 13 Armoured Regiment

2IC: Second-in-command

AC: Armoured Corps

ACG: Annual Contingency Grant

ACR: Annual Confidential Report

AFV: Armoured Fighting Vehicle

AG: Adjutant General

AHQ: Army Headquarters

ARN: Army Reserve North

ARS: Army Reserve South

BPET: Battle Physical Efficiency Test

BSF: Border Security Force

CAFVD: Central Armoured Fighting Vehicles Depot

CDA: Controller of Defence Accounts

CGI: Corrugated Galvanized Iron

CIA: Central Intelligence Agency

CIH: Central India Horse (an Armoured Regiment)

CILQ: Compensation in Lieu of Quarters

COD: Central Ordnance Depot

CRO: Chief Record Officer

CSD: Canteen Stores Department

DAC: Director Armoured Corps

DDMO[B]: Deputy Director Military Operations Branch

DGMO: Director General Military Operations

DMR: Driving and Maintenance Regiment

DRDO: Defence Research & Development Organisation

DTL: Dashing Troop Leader

EME (ops): Electric and Mechanical Engineers (Operations)

ETA: Estimated Time of Arrival

FOO: Forward Observation Officer

FSMO: Field Service Marching Order

GE: Garrison Engineer

GHQ: General Headquarters

GOC-in-C: General Officer Commanding-in-Chief

GPS: Global Positioning System

GS: General Service

IAAS: Indian Audit & Accounts Service

IDAS: Indian Defence Accounts Service

IMA: Indian Military Academy

IO: Intelligence Officer

ISI: Inter-Services Agency

JIC: Joint Intelligence Committee

KGB: Komitet Gosudarstvennoy Bezopasnosti

KLP: Key Location Point

LRW: Light Repair Workshop

MC: Master of Ceremonies

MEA: Ministry of External Affairs

MID: Mention in Despatches

MIRC: Mechanised Infantry Regimental Centre

MoD: Ministry of Defence

MS: Military Secretary

NMB: No Move Before

OC: Officer Commanding

OIC: Other Indian Classes

OR: Other Ranks

ORBAT: Order of Battle

PBG: President's Bodyguard

PCK: Previous Course Knowledge

PMC: President Mess Committee

QM: Quartermaster

RAPID: Reorganized Army Plains Infantry Division

RAW: Research & Analysis Wing

RHQ: Regimental Headquarters

RM: Risaldar Major

RSO: Regimental Signal Officer

SD4: Staff Duties (Section 4)

SIC: South Indian Classes

SOPs: Standard Operating Procedures

TRH: Tent Replacement Hut

WE: War Establishment

WET: War Equipment Tables

WILCO: Will Comply

i. Wedding photograph 7 March 1977. Seated (L to R): Madhu with son Rohit, Mrs Sheila Mehta (mother), wife Jayshree, the author, Kukkie. Standing: Shamsher, Uncle KD, Surinder, Rajinder, Minoo and Kusum holding twins, with Narinder in the middle

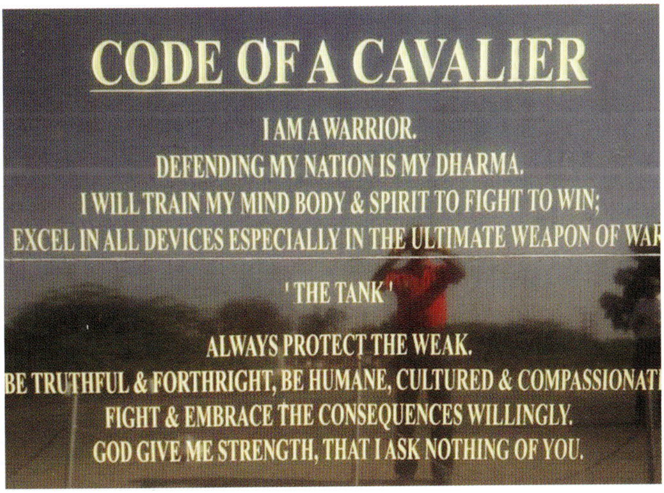

ii. Code of a Cavalier

iii. The author Colonel B. S. Mehta on his farewell visit to the Sikh Squadron

iv. First group photograph of the officers who helped in the raising of 13 Armoured Regiment at Ahmednagar (1985)

v. Colonel B. S. Mehta congratulates Lieutenant Colonel Randhir Singh after handing over command of 13 Armoured Regiment on 9 June 1987

vi. Colonel B. S.Mehta, Commandant 13 Armoured Regiment, addressing a conference

vii. Officers and JCOs of 13 Armoured Regiment celebrating the successful completion of the raising and being declared 'Fit For War' after test exercise conducted with troops and an administrative inspection by Lieutenant General Kler, Commandant ACCS, Ahmednagar

viii. Smt. Pratibha Devisingh Patil, Former President of India, with Commandant Colonel Umesh Varma (standing on her right) along with serving and retired officers and ladies of 13 Armoured Regiment on the occasion of Standard Presentation to the Regiment

ix. 16 March 1985: The regimental flag was hoisted at Ahmednagar at 1050 hrs by Lieutenant Colonel B. S. Mehta in the presence of 14 officers, 22 JCOs and 168 ORs after invoking the prayers performed by the pandit, granthi, maulvi and priest

x. Major General Shailjanand Jha (Retd) receiving the Param Vishisht Seva Medal from the President of India Sh. Ram Nath Kovind on 30 May 2022

RESTRICTED

PRESIDENT'S STANDARDS - 2010

GOC-IN-C, SWC UNIT CITATION 2019

13 ARMOURED REGIMENT

SPECIAL ORDER OF THE DAY BY COL PIYUSH VERMA, SM COMMANDANT

c/o 56 APO	MONDAY	22 AUG 2022

COMPLIMENTARY

Col Patial Nitish Comdt 7th Light Cavalry	Col Piyush Verma, SM Comdt 13 Armd Regt	Col Vishal Singh Comdt 60 Armd Regt

1. It is a matter of immense pride and honour for the "**TRISKAIDECA FRATERNITY" to proclaim that three Cavaliers of this Kavachit Risala** are presently spearheading the chariots of three finest Regiments ranging from one amongst the oldest to one amongst the youngest Regiments of Armd Corps. The occasion is a rare feat in itself and would add another page of glory to the annals of rich heritage of Triskadeca History.

2. We owe this achievement to the strong foundation laid down by our veterans and indefatigable dedication exhibited by **Team 13** which aptly reflects the rich traditions, ethos and Espirit-de-corps that the regiment has imbibed since its raising. We are sanguine that this is only a harbinger of many such laurels that shall follow in future.

3. On behalf of Brig BS Bisht, Col of the Regt, we vow to uphold the standards set by the Regt and will leave no stone unturned in achieving the pinnacle of success in every arena of professionalism.

'TERA SAB TERA'
-VEER BHOGYA VASUNDHARA-

(Piyush Verma)
Colonel
Commandant

RESTRICTED

xi. A Special Order of the Day in honour of the Triskaideca fraternity

xii. Brigadier B. S. Mehta presenting his book 'The Burning Chaffees' to General Bipin Rawat, COAS

xiii. The author shares a moment with his bull mastiff, Trigger